A
GILBERT & SULLIVAN
DICTIONARY

Da Capo Press Music Reprint Series

GENERAL EDITOR

FREDERICK FREEDMAN

VASSAR COLLEGE

A
GILBERT & SULLIVAN
DICTIONARY

Compiled by
GEORGE E. DUNN

DA CAPO PRESS • NEW YORK • 1971

A Da Capo Press Reprint Edition

This Da Capo Press edition of *A Gilbert & Sullivan Dictionary*
is an unabridged republication of the first edition published in
New York in 1936. It is reprinted by special arrangement with
Oxford University Press.

Library of Congress Catalog Card Number 72-125070

ISBN 0-306-70007-7

Published by Da Capo Press, Inc.
A Subsidiary of Plenum Publishing Corporation
227 West 17th Street, New York, New York 10011

A
GILBERT & SULLIVAN
DICTIONARY

A
GILBERT & SULLIVAN
DICTIONARY

compiled by

GEORGE E. DUNN

"Factus" of "Musical Opinion"

NEW YORK

OXFORD UNIVERSITY PRESS

1936

FIRST PUBLISHED IN 1936

PRINTED IN GREAT BRITAIN BY
UNWIN BROTHERS LTD., WOKING

DEDICATED TO AN
"ELSIE MAYNARD"

FOREWORD

This GILBERT AND SULLIVAN DICTIONARY is intended for the use primarily of amateur players and producers, and secondarily of all who are interested in the immortal series of Savoy Operas.

As it seems a reasonable supposition that artists cannot impart full expression to their "lines" unless they know the meaning of all the words contained in them, this work is directed mainly to the attempt to explain every obscure word, phrase, and allusion to be found in the libretti, to give some account of the various classical and topical names of persons, places, and incidents; and to supply approximate translations of all foreign and colloquial words.

In addition, all the characters are given, with their original creators, and also the understudies, deputies, and successors of such parts in the original productions. Particulars are also given of all the operas themselves and their first productions, of the theatres at which they were produced, and many other matters connected with the presentation of the operas from 1875 to the close of the late Mrs. D'Oyly Carte's tenure of the Savoy Theatre in 1909. Thus the various revivals at the Savoy Theatre up to the conclusion of this period of thirty-four years are included.

This third of a century of Savoy Opera may be divided, roughly speaking, into three periods, representing the three marked changes in the personnel of

7

the stock company. Naturally these divisions are to some extent illusory, for the company was not, strictly speaking, changed, but gradually metamorphosed, and there are many overlappings. Nevertheless, in course of time, a new company was almost imperceptibly formed, and they were sufficiently definite to be considered as three groups, as suggested.

As the succession of chief comedians, around each of whom a company was built up, was the most marked feature, these three periods may be considered the Grossmith Period, the Passmore Period, and the Workman Period. Curiously enough, the alterations in one other type of character were so synchronous that a sub-title might almost be given as regards the chief soubrette. Thus the three periods might be reckoned as the Grossmith–Jessie Bond, the Passmore–Florence Perry, and the Workman–Jessie Rose. Several principals, of course, can be included in more than one of these periods, such as Rosina Brandram and (Sir) Henry Lytton, while Rutland Barrington figured in all three.

The Grossmith Period was from 1875 to 1889, that is, from the production of *Trial by Jury* to *The Yeomen of the Guard*. (Mr. Grossmith, however, did not actually appear until the production of *The Sorcerer*.)

The Passmore Period was from 1890 to 1901, from *The Gondoliers* to *The Grand Duke* and various revivals. (Mr. Passmore did not actually appear until the production of Conan Doyle, Barrie, and Ernest Ford's *Jane Annie* shortly before the production of *Utopia Ltd.*)

8

The Workman Period was from 1901 to 1909, which witnessed the second series of revivals. (Mr. Workman first appeared as Ben Hashbaz in *The Grand Duke*.)

An apology may appear to be due for the inclusion, in this book, of references which would seem to be too obvious to be necessary, such as Camberwell or Pickford. Such references are included for the benefit of provincial, overseas and American enthusiasts, to whom a number of place names and topical London matters may be unfamiliar.

THE AUTHOR

LIST OF ABBREVIATIONS

circa	.	about	*Naut.*	.	Nautical
e.g.	.	for example	Pat.	.	*Patience*
Fr.	.	French	Pin.	.	*Pinafore*
G.	.	*Gondoliers*	Pir.	.	*Pirates*
G.D.	.	*Grand Duke*	P.I.	.	*Princess Ida*
Geom.	.	Geometry	*q.v.*	.	which see
Ger.	.	German	R.	.	*Ruddigore*
Gr.	.	Greek	*Rhet.*	.	Rhetoric
Gr. Myth.	.	Greek Mythology	*Rom. Myth.*		Roman Mythology
I.	.	*Iolanthe*			
It.	.	Italian	S.	.	*Sorcerer*
Lat.	.	Latin	T. by J.	.	*Trial by Jury*
M.	.	*Mikado*	*Trig.*	.	Trigonometry
Math.	.	Mathematics	U.	.	*Utopia Limited*
Mil.	.	Military	Y.	.	*Yeomen of the Guard*

GILBERT AND SULLIVAN DICTIONARY

A

Abudah ("Our Abudah chests, each containing a patent Hag." S. 1).—A wealthy merchant of Baghdad, in Ridley's *Tales of the Genii*. He seeks a talisman from an old hag, who gives him one symbolic of conscience, which haunts him continually.

Aceldama ("This black Aceldama of sorrow." Pat. 1) —In a general sense, a field of blood; specifically, the potter's field bought with blood money by Judas Iscariot. As its general use is quite common, there need be no sense of irreverence at its introduction into a comic opera. Pronounced "Ass-el-dáh-ma."

A-cockbill ("What's brought you all a-cockbill?" R. 1.).—Having one yard-arm longer than the other. Hence, distraught. (*Naut.*)

ADA (P.I.).—Girl Graduate at Castle Adamant, who acts as military bandmistress in Act. III.

Agamemnon ("My appearance as King Agamemnon in a Louis Quatorze wig." G.D. 1).—King of Mycenae and Commander-in-Chief of the Greek forces before Troy. He was murdered by his wife Clytemnestra. It is an example of Gilbert's whimsicality to assign so tragic a part to the *chief comedian* of Ernest Dummkopf's Company.

Ahrimanes ("or you or I must yield up his life to Ahrimanes." S. 2).—In Zoroastrian (Persian) theology, the Spirit of Evil, as opposed to Ormuzd, the Spirit of Good. Analogous to our notion of the Devil, but with the difference that the two opposing spirits were reckoned as equally powerful. Pronounced "Ah-ri-máh-nees."

Aiaiah (I. 2).—An ejaculation of grief by the Fairies at Iolanthe's death sentence. Presumably suggested by the Greek αἰαῖ, "Woe is me."

AINSWORTH, F.—Appeared in the original production of *Patience* as Colonel Calverley.

ALEXIS (S.).—Of the Grenadier Guards. Son of Sir Marmaduke Pointdextre, and betrothed to Aline.

Algernon (Pat.).—The Christian name which Gilbert originally gave to Grosvenor. It was altered to Archibald in deference to the wish of one of the Westminster family whose name was Algernon Grosvenor, who later became Lord Ebury. Curiously enough, it appears once in error in the Chatto and Windus edition of the libretto.

ALHAMBRA DEL BOLERO, DON (G.).—The Grand Inquisitor of Spain. See "Grandee" and "Hidalgo."

ALINE (S.).—Daughter of Lady Sangazure, and betrothed to Alexis.

ALLEN, G. B.—One of the directors of the Comedy Opera Company, and assistant conductor during the run of *The Sorcerer*. See Notes on the original production of *Pinafore*.

14

Alliteration.—Three examples of this literary device, taken at random, are:—

"The lucid lake of liquid love" (S. 1).

"Blushing bride of ever-blowing beauty" (Pir. 1).

"Dull, dark dock; pestilential prison; life-long lock; short, sharp shock; cheap and chippy chopper; big black block" (M. 1).

"All that glitters is not gold" (Pin. 2).—Adapted from "All that glisters is not gold" (*Merchant of Venice*, Act II, Sc. 7). Similar phrases, predating Shakespeare, are to be found in the works of Lydgate and Spenser; also by Middleton, Dryden, and George Herbert.

"Altogether" ("something like the 'altogether.'" G.D. 2).—Artists' term for the nude, popularized by its use in George du Maurier's novel *Trilby*, which had been published a year before the production of *The Grand Duke*.

Amaranthine ("Quivering on amaranthine asphodel." Pat. 1).—Although an amaranth has nothing to do with an asphodel, this adjective is not so inconsequent as might appear. It may also mean "that which does not fade quickly," a characteristic of both an amaranth, a flower of the Love-lies-bleeding species, and an asphodel (daffodil).

Amaryllis ("So come, Amaryllis." R. 1).—Typifying a pastoral sweetheart. It is to be found in Theocritus and Virgil, but the best-known example is "To sport with Amaryllis in the shade," from Milton's *Lycidas*.

Ambrose, Hugh ("The Merrie Jestes of Hugh Ambrose." Y. 2).—The source of Jack Point's *original* light humour. Ambrose was a real person, who wrote such a book in Tudor times.

Amorous Dove ("O amorous dove." I. 2).—Ovid, the Roman amatory poet, likens himself to a dove. See "Ovidius Naso."

Anacreon ("You should read Anacreon." P.I. 2).— The famous Greek poet of Taos, *circa* 500 B.C. He is said to have died of choking by a grape pip.

ANDERSEN ("A fairy, from Andersen's libr*a*ry." I. 1).—Hans Andersen, the Danish writer of Fairy Tales.

ANGELA, THE LADY (Pat.).—One of the principal Rapturous Maidens. In the end, she allies herself to Major Murgatroyd. It is important to note this as, until the final Quintet, everything points to her choosing the Colonel.

Angelina (T. by J.).—The name of the Plaintiff. See "Edwin and Angelina."

Animals.—The animals mentioned in the operas are: ape (P.I. 2); ass (P.I. 3; Y. 1); baboon (G.D. 1); bat (R. 2; G.D. 1); black and tan (terrier) (Pat. 2); bull (Pin. 2; Y. 2); bull-dog (P.I. 2); cat (Pin. 2); dog (R. 1); elephant (P.I. 2); fawn (U. 2); filly (R. 1); fox (U. 2); guinea-pig (S. 1; R. 2); horse (I. 2; P.I. 2; G. 1); hound (U. 2); lamb (Pin. 2); lion (Y. 1); mouse (Y. 2); opossum (R. 1); oxen (R. 1); pig (P.I. 2); pony (R. 1; roe (M. 2); sheep (Pin. 2; R. 1); squirrel (R. 1; Y. 2); swine (R. 1); tiger (U. 2); tiger-cat (R. 2); weazel (P.I. 2); white mice (Pat. 2).

Annabella (S.).—The Christian name of Lady Sang-azure.

Annibale (G.).—One of the Gondoliers.

Antonio (G.).—One of the Gondoliers. The part was offered to, and declined by, Richard Temple.

"Apologetic Statesmen" (M. 1).—When Ko-Ko's song is encored, this line is usually followed by some dumb show, in caricature of some well-known politicians, such as the eyeglass of Sir Austen Chamberlain, the moustache of Mr. Ramsay MacDonald, the pipe of Mr. Baldwin, the golf of the late Lord Balfour, and other characteristics of any prominent statesman of the period.

Apostrophe (i. "I find some satisfaction in apostrophe like this." S. 1; ii. "You are interrupting an apostrophe, Sir." M. 1).—A figure of speech, wherein the speaker suddenly changes from the indefinite third person to the definite second person. Both of the above quotations refer to correct examples of this rhetorical form.

Aquinas, Thomas (Pat. 1).—Mentioned in the Colonel's song. The famous Dominican friar of the thirteenth century, who was largely responsible for the Inquisition. His festival is on March 7th.

Arac (P.I.).—The chief of Gama's three sons.

Arcadian Vale ("Peckham an Arcadian Vale." T. by J.).—Arcadia was a beautiful district of Greece in the heart of the Peloponnessus, where everyone dwelt peacefully and happily. Used as a symbol of ideal rusticity. The first scene of *Iolanthe* is an Arcadian landscape.

Archbishop of Canterbury ("My lord was the Archbishop of Canterbury." Y. 1).—Jack Point's master was either John Morton, Henry Dean, or William Warham. It could not have been the most famous Archbishop in Henry VIII's reign, Thomas Cranmer, for he was not elevated to the Primacy until after the death of Sir Richard Cholmondeley (*q.v.*).

Ariston ("A *recherché* cold ἄριστον." G.D. 2).—A late breakfast or early luncheon in ancient Greece, analogous to the Roman prandium and the Indian tiffin. Pronounced "a-riss-ton."

Aristophanes ("The *Frogs* of Aristophanes." Pir. 1).—The famous comic dramatist of Greece. Mentioned also by Lady Psyche. (P.I. 2.)

ARNOLD, GRACE.—Appeared in the original production of *Iolanthe* as Fleta.

Artists.—The artists mentioned in the operas are: Fra Angelica (Pat. 2); Botticelli (Pat. 2); Gerhard Dhow (Pir. 1); (Sir) Luke Fyldes (U. 2); (Sir) John Millais (U. 2); Raphael (Pir. 1); and Zoffany (Pir. 1).

ASHTON, KNIGHT.—Appeared in the original production of *Trial by Jury* as the Defendant.

Asinorum pons ("That *asinorum pons* I have crossed without assistance." U. 2).—*Pons asinorum* (*Lat.*), the "Asses' bridge," is the schoolboy name for the 5th Proposition of the First Book of Euclid.

Ass, A live ("A live ass is better than a dead lion."
Y. 1).—Phoebe is misquoting a verse from Ecclesi-
astes, which runs, "A living dog is better than a
dead lion."

Associate (T. by J.).—He sits below the Judge's
bench and hands up a reference book from Counsel
to his Lordship, a function sometimes undertaken
by an Usher.

Attic ("Every dining-room was Attic." G.D. 2).—
Pertaining to Attica, otherwise to Athens, its
principal city. The modern meaning of "attic," a
room immediately below the roof, is derived from
the same source, the ancient attic being a low storey
above the main order of the Greek façade.

AUGARDE, AMY.—This famous player (later) of
Lydia Hawthorne in *Dorothy* appeared in the
original production of *Ruddigore* as Mad Margaret.

Aurora ("As Aurora gilds the sky." S. 1).—The Roman
goddess of the morning. Hence, daybreak, sunrise.

Authors.—The authors and playwrights mentioned in
the operas are: Hugh Ambrose (Y. 2); Hans
Andersen (I. 1); Aristophanes (Pir. 1); Erasmus
Beadle (Pat. 1); Dion Boucicault (Pat. 1); Darwin
(P.I. 2); Defoe (Pat. 1); Dickens (Pat. 1; U. 2);
Fielding (Pat. 1); Hipparchus (P.I. 2); Juvenal
(P.I. 2); Macaulay (Pat. 1); Thackeray, (Pat. 1;
U. 2); Anthony Trollope (Pat. 1); and Martin
Tupper (Pat. 1).

B

Bab Ballads.—These humorous poems, constituting Gilbert's first important publication, were issued in 1861, when the author was but twenty-five years old. Several of them have served as germs of the plots of the operas.

Backwardation ("... and also Backwardation." U. 1). —A financial term, meaning a premium paid by a seller to a buyer of stock in consideration of the former being allowed to postpone delivery.

Bailey ("At the Bailey." T. by J.).—The Old Bailey, officially known as the Central Criminal Court, situated at Newgate. Referred to later in the same work as "Ancient Bailey."

BAKER, MILDRED.—Created the part of Olga in *The Grand Duke*.

BALDWIN, ALICE.—Appeared in the original production of *The Gondoliers* as Gianetta.

Bandy ("No need to bandy aught that appertains to you." P.I. 1).—Cyril makes use of Gama's expression "to bandy words" and turns it into an impertinent allusion to the King's bandy legs.

Bank Holiday ("Jolly Bank Holiday every day young man." Pat. 2).—The general observance of the four annual Bank Holidays had been in force only ten years before the production of *Patience*, brought about mainly through the exertions of Sir John Lubbock, later Lord Avebury. In *Ruddigore*, Sir Ruthven excuses his non-commission of a crime on the Monday on the grounds that it was a Bank Holiday, presumably, judging from the poppies carried by Mad Margaret, the first Monday in August.

Baptisto (G.).—The Christian name of Palmieri, the reputed father of Marco and Giuseppe.

Barataria (G.).—The name of the island kingdom, where Marco and Giuseppe reign jointly, is derived from Sancho Panza's city in Cervantes' *Don Quixote*.

Baring ("Ever so many are taken by Rothschild and Baring." I. 2).—From the Lord Chancellor's Song. The banking firm of Baring was founded by Sir Francis Baring at the end of the eighteenth century. Direct descendants hold the titles of Lords Ashburton, Cromer, Northbrook, and Revelstoke.

BARKER, RICHARD.—General manager of the third period of the original production of *Trial by Jury*, and, later, D'Oyly Carte's henchman for several years. See *"Pinafore* Riot."

BARLOW, BILLIE.—Appeared in the original production of *The Pirates of Penzance* as Kate. Later became a popular variety artist.

BARNARD, CECIL.—Appeared in the original production of *The Gondoliers* as the Duke of Plaza-Toro and Don Alhambra.

BARNETT, ALICE.—Created the parts of Lady Jane in *Patience* and the Queen of the Fairies in *Iolanthe*. Also appeared in the original production of *The Pirates of Penzance* as Ruth.

B

BARNETT, F.—Appeared in the original production of *The Yeomen of the Guard* as Leonard, and of *The Gondoliers* as Francesco.

BARRE, SIR BAILEY (U.).—One of the Six Flowers of Progress, representing the Law.

BARRINGTON, RUTLAND.—Created the parts of Dr. Daly in *The Sorcerer*; Captain Corcoran in *Pinafore*; the Sergeant of Police in *The Pirates of Penzance*; Archibald Grosvenor in *Patience*; Mount-ararat in *Iolanthe*; King Hildebrand in *Princess Ida*; Pooh-Bah in *The Mikado*; Sir Despard Murgatroyd in *Ruddigore*; Giuseppe in *The Gondoliers*; King Paramount in *Utopia Ltd.*; and Ludwig in *The Grand Duke*. As in revivals (which are not generally considered in this book) he played the Judge in *Trial by Jury* and Wilfred Shadbolt in *The Yeomen of the Guard*, he holds the record of being the only Savoyard to play in all the thirteen works. He does not, however, hold the record for the greatest number of parts played at the Savoy Theatre, that being easily held by Sir Henry Lytton (*q.v.*).

Basingstoke (R. 2).—The word, "teeming with hidden meaning," which Mad Margaret selects to be used to bring her to a calm frame of mind.

Beadle of Burlington (Pat. 1).—Mentioned in the Colonel's Song. Often thought, erroneously, to refer to the dignified beadle who used to stand at the Burlington Arcade. It alludes to Erasmus F. Beadle, of Burlington, New Jersey. He was the inventor of the "dime novel," an American equivalent to our "penny dreadful." He made a large fortune out of this cheap literature, and died in 1861.

"Beard the lion in his den" (I. 2).—A verbatim quotation from Scott's *Marmion*—"Dar'st thou beard the lion in his den, The Douglas in his hall."

Beauchamp Tower (Y.).—The precise position of this tower would be the auditorium side of St. Peter ad Vincula. Fairfax's entry would, correctly, be across the front of the chapel door, as it is structurally impossible to get from the tower to the rear of the chapel. Phoebe's reference to his taking exercise is quite accurate, for the top of the Beauchamp was used by prisoners as an exercise ground.

BECKET, BOB (Pin.)—Carpenter's mate on board the *Pinafore*. Like most of the crew, the name has a nautical meaning. A becket is a ring or loop of metal or rope for holding spars.

BEDFORD, MR.—Appeared in the original production of *Trial by Jury* as the Foreman.

Belgrave Square ("Hearts just as pure and fair may beat in Belgrave Square." I. 1).—This fashionable square in the West End of London is so called from one of the titles of the ground landlord, the Duke of Westminster.

Belgravian airies (U. 1).—Referring to the old-fashioned areas in the basement of the houses of the Georgian and Victorian period which are to be seen in Belgravia, and other districts in the West End of London. They were popularly supposed to be the favourite locale for flirtations between the iron railings by domestic servants and soldiers, tradesmen, and policemen.

Bell of St. Peter's (Y.).—The chapel of St. Peter ad

Vincula adjoins the place of execution on Tower Green, and the bell was always tolled, whether the execution took place on Tower Green or on Tower Hill. Care should be taken that the "bell is tolled" from the O.P. side, and not by the prompter.

BELL, MAY.—Created the part of Melene in *Utopia Ltd.*

Belted Earl ("Fled . . . belted earls before me." S. 1). —A cincture is part of the official attire of an earl.

BENTHAM, GEORGE.—Created the part of Alexis in *The Sorcerer*.

Ben venuto (G. 1) (It.).—Literally "well come," i.e. "welcome."

BERNARD, ANNIE.—Created the part of Inez in *The Gondoliers*. Appeared also in the original production of *The Mikado* as Katisha, and of *The Yeomen of the Guard* as Dame Carruthers.

BERTHA (G.D.).—One of the girls in Dummkopf's theatrical company.

BEVERLEY, MR.—The painter of the scenery of the original *Sorcerer*, and one of the most eminent scenic artists of the day.

BILLINGTON, FRED.—Appeared in the original production of *Ruddigore* as Sir Despard. For thirty years he was the chief player of the "Barrington" parts in the No. 1 touring company.

Binnacle ("A clear conscience for your binnacle light." R. 1).—A stand on the top of the compass box where a lantern may be placed. (*Naut.*)

Binomial Theorem ("About binomial theorem I'm teeming with a lot o' news." Pir. 1).—The law of the formation of any power of a binomial, which means an expression of two terms connected by the signs plus or minus. It was first expounded by Sir Isaac Newton.

Birds.—The birds mentioned in the operas are: carrion (crow) (Y. 1; U. 2); cock (Y. 2); dove (turtle dove) (I. 2; Y. 1; U. 1); eagle (U. 2); goose (G. 1); grouse (I. 1; U. 2); hawk (Pat. 2); hen (P.I. 1); jackdaw (Pin. 2); nightingale (Philomel) (Pin. 1; U. 2); owl (Y. 1); peacock (popinjay) (Pin. 2; Y. 1); skylark (Y. 1); sparrow (I. 1; U. 2); stork (Pin. 2); swan (G. 1); tom-tit (R. 1).

Birmingham (R. 2).—The word Sir Ruthven uses to calm Mad Margaret, in mistake for "Basingstoke."

Bismarck ("Genius of Bismarck devising a plan." Pat. 1).—From the Colonel's Song. Prince Bismarck, the German Chancellor, was at the height of his fame at the time of the production of *Patience*.

BLACKMORE, H. ENES.—Created the part of Sir Bailey Barre in *Utopia Ltd*.

Black Sheep ("Black sheep grow in every fold." Pin. 2).—The origin of the saying, "There is a black sheep in every fold," is doubtful. But, as far back as 1550, is to be found the saying, "The black shepe is a perylous beast."

BLANCHE, LADY (P.I.).—Professor of Abstract Science and mother of Melissa. She succeeds, in the end, to the Headship of Princess Ida's University.

"Blood is thick, but water's thin" (I. 2).—Paraphrase of "Blood is thicker than water." See John Ray's *Collection of English Proverbs*, 1742.

BLUSHINGTON, MR. (U.).—One of the Six Flowers of Progress, representing the County Councillor. His name and his references to music halls reflect the movement in 1893 to close the Promenade at the Empire Theatre, chiefly through the activities of Mrs. Ormiston Chant.

BOBSTAY, BILL (Pin.).—Boatswain's mate. A bobstay is a rope or chain to confine the bowsprit downward to the stem or cutwater. (*Naut.*)

Bolero ("Dance a cachucha, fandango, bolero," G. 2). —A Spanish dance invented by Zerezo in 1780, so slightly anticipated in Barataria, the opera taking place in 1750. A slow, minuet-like measure, danced by two persons only. Bolero was Don Alhambra's patronymic.

Bombazine ("rusty bombazine." I. 1).—A fabric, usually black, made of mixed silk and worsted. It is used chiefly for old-fashioned mourning dresses, and for the black gowns worn by graduates, undergraduates, vergers, and law court officials.

Bonaparte ("When Wellington thrashed Bonaparte." I. 2).—From Mountararat's Song. Napoleon discarded the "u" in Buonaparte when First Consul.

BOND, JESSIE.—Created the parts of Hebe in *Pinafore*; Lady Angela in *Patience*; Iolanthe in *Iolanthe*; Melissa in *Princess Ida*; Pitti-Sing in *The Mikado*; Mad Margaret in *Ruddigore*; Phoebe in *The Yeomen of the Guard*; and Tessa in *The Gondoliers*. She missed playing the part of Edith in *The Pirates of Penzance* at the Savoy Theatre, as she was playing it in America.

BOND, NEVA.—Created the part of Isabel in *The Pirates of Penzance*.

BOSANQUET, MR.—Appeared in the original production of *Pinafore* as Bill Bobstay.

Botticellian ("How Botticellian!" Pat. 2).—In the style of Sandro Botticelli, the famous painter of the Renaissance. He died in Florence in 1510.

Boucicault ("The pathos of Paddy, as rendered by Boucicault." Pat. 1).—From the Colonel's Song. Dion Boucicault, the father of Dion Boucicault, Junior, the father-in-law of Irene Vanbrugh, and the grandfather of Dion Calthrop, wrote or adapted 140 plays, the best known being *London Assurance*, *Arrah-na-Pogue*, and *The Colleen Bawn*.

BOVILL, FRED.—Created the part of Pish-Tush in *The Mikado*. Appeared also in the original production of the same opera as Pooh-Bah.

Bowdlerized ("You will get them Bowdlerized." P.I. 2).—An expurgated edition, omitting anything likely to offend modern taste. From Thomas Bowdler, who, in 1818, issued such an edition of Shakespeare.

BOWLEY, GEORGE.—Created the part of Mr. Bunthorne's Solicitor in *Patience*.

BOYD, MR.—Created the part of the Second Citizen in *The Yeomen of the Guard*.

B

BRACY, HENRY.—Created the part of Hilarion in *Princess Ida*.

BRAHAM, LEONORA.—Created the parts of Patience in *Patience*; Phyllis in *Iolanthe*; Princess Ida in *Princess Ida*; Yum-Yum in *The Mikado*; and Rose Maybud in *Ruddigore*.

Brain pan ("Why a cook's brain pan is like an overwound clock?" Y. 1).—A brain pan has nothing specially to do with a cook. It is merely a colloquialism for the human skull.

BRANDRAM, ROSINA.—Created the parts of Lady Blanche in *Princess Ida*; Katisha in *The Mikado*; Dame Hannah in *Ruddigore*; Dame Carruthers in *The Yeomen of the Guard*; The Duchess of Plaza-Toro in *The Gondoliers*; Lady Sophy in *Utopia Ltd.*; and The Baroness von Krakenfeldt in *The Grand Duke*. Appeared also in the original productions of *The Sorcerer* as Lady Sangazure; of *Pinafore* as Buttercup; of *The Pirates of Penzance* as Kate; of *Patience* as Lady Jane; and of *Iolanthe* as the Queen of the Fairies. She was thus the only principal to appear in *all* the original productions at the Savoy Theatre, and the only lady to appear in the original productions of the entire series except *Trial by Jury*.

Bridget (Y. 1).—The Christian name of Elsie Maynard's mother.

Brindisi (S. 1). (*It.*).—A drinking song. In this instance, it is a teetotal drinking song.

BROMLEY, NELLIE.—Created the part of the Plaintiff in *Trial by Jury*. She later became Mrs. Stuart-Wortley.

BROWNE, WALTER.—Appeared in the original production of *Patience* as Colonel Calverley.

BROWNLOW, WALLACE.—Created the parts of Sir Richard Cholmondeley in *The Yeomen of the Guard*, and of Luiz in *The Gondoliers*. Also appeared in the original production of *Ruddigore* as Sir Roderic, and of *The Gondoliers* as Giuseppe.

"Bulls are but inflated frogs" (Pin. 2).—From Aesop's Fable of the Frog who burst herself trying to inflate her body to the size of a bull.

Bunthorne, Reginald (Pat.).—A fleshly poet. In appearance he was a caricature of J. M. Whistler, the artist. See "Grosvenor Gallery."

"*Buon' giorno, Signorine!*" etc. (G. 1).—The literal translation of these eighteen Italian lines is as follows:—

> Giuseppe and Marco. Good morning, young ladies!
> Girls. Dearest gondoliers! We are country maidens!
> Giu. and Marc. Your humble servants! For whom are these flowers—These most beautiful flowers?
> Girls. For you, good gentlemen, O most excellent!
> Giu. and Marc. O Heaven!
> Girls. Good morning, cavaliers!
> Giu. and Marc. We are gondoliers. Lady, I love thee!
> Girls. We are country maidens.
> Giu. and Marc. Ladies! Country maidens!

GIRLS. Cavaliers!

GIU. AND MARC. Gondoliers! Poor Gondoliers!

BURBANK, MR.—Created the part of the 12th Baronet, Sir Conrad Murgatroyd, in *Ruddigore*. Appeared in the original production of *The Gondoliers* as Annibale.

Burgling, A- ("When the enterprising burglar's not a-burgling." Pir. 2).—Gilbert was the first author of note to use this verb.

Burlesques.—Two of the operas were the subject of burlesque. In May 1882 was produced at the Opera Comique a burlesque entitled *The Wreck of the "Pinafore."* It was written by Horace Lingard and composed by Luscombe Searrelle. In 1888 John L. Toole produced at Toole's Theatre a burlesque on *Ruddigore* entitled *Ruddy George*.

BURVILLE, ALICE.—Appeared in the original production of *Pinafore* as Josephine.

BUTTERCUP, LITTLE (Pin.).—A Portsmouth bumboat woman, who holds the secret of Captain Corcoran's and Ralph Rackstraw's birth. A bumboat is a clumsy vessel used for conveying provisions to ships lying in port or in dock. Little Buttercup's real name is Mrs. Cripps.

Byfleet, Sir Martin (Y. 1).—One of Fairfax's fellow-prisoners in the Beauchamp Tower. He and all the other prisoners mentioned by Dame Carruthers are purely fictitious.

C

Cachucha (G. 2).—A dance somewhat akin to the
Bolero, but quicker and accompanied with castanets. It is danced in couples, and included in its
features are the completion of a circle by means of
four quarter turns, and the backward glissade of
alternate feet at the second and fourth of the four
sections of the measure. Sullivan's music, though,
melodically original, faithfully follows the tradi-
tional style and rhythm.

Caesar ("The genius strategic of Caesar. . . ." Pat. 1).
—From the Colonel's Song.

Calomel ("All can be set right with calomel." Pat. 1).
—Chloride of mercury.

CALVERLEY, COL. (Pat.).—The O.C. the Squadron of
the 35th Dragoon Guards. He eventually is
betrothed to Lady Saphir.

CALYNX (U.).—The Utopian Vice-Chamberlain.

Camberwell ("Camberwell became a bower." T. by J.).
—From the Counsel's speech. A populous district
in the South-East of London.

CAMERON, ELSIE.—Appeared in the original production of *Ruddigore* as Dame Hannah; and of *The
Gondoliers* as the Duchess of Plaza-Toro.

CAMPBELL, MR.—Created the part of the Foreman
of the Jury in *Trial by Jury*. Also appeared in the
original production of the same work as the
Defendant.

C

Canaille ("Base canaille! That word is French!" I. 1).—
Rabble, riff-raff. Gilbert uses an Anglicized pro-
nunciation of the word, making it rhyme with
"Style."

Capstan ("We'll heave the capstan round." M. 1).—
A vertical cylinder revolving on a spindle for
moving weights. It is used chiefly aboard for raising
the anchor, and ashore for drawing up a boat to
dry land. It is usually man-operated, each one
walking round the capstan, pushing a lever fitted
into one of the sockets. (*Naut.*)

Captain Shaw ("Oh, Captain Shaw, type of true love
kept under." I. 2).—Sir Eyre Massey Shaw, a
famous Chief of the London Fire Brigade in the
'eighties. He was an inveterate playgoer, and was
present to hear this reference to him on the opening
night of *Iolanthe*.

Caradoc, Sir ("I know our mythic history, King
Arthur's and Sir Caradoc's." Pir. 1).—One of the
Knights of King Arthur's Round Table. He was
said to be the only one whose wife was not unfaith-
ful. See "The Boy and the Mantle," from Percy's
Reliques.

CARLINGFORD, ROSE.—Appeared in the original
production of *Iolanthe* as the Queen of the Fairies.

CARLTON, MR.—Created the part of Viscount
Mentone in *The Grand Duke*.

Carole (Y. 1).—One of Jack Point's dances. Really a
composite French dance, wherein several people
sing and dance in a circle.

Caroline (G.D.).—The Christian name of the Baroness von Krakenfeldt.

CARR, LILIAN.—Appeared in the original production of *Princess Ida* as Ada. Her name appears in the published programme as the creator of the part, but the originator was Miss Twynam. Also appeared in the original production of *The Mikado* as Pitti-Sing.

CARRITTE, MISS.—Appeared in the original production of *The Gondoliers* as Gianetta.

CARRUTHERS, DAME (Y.).—Housekeeper to the Tower. Discovered by her in his plot to effect Colonel Fairfax's escape, Sergeant Meryll allies himself to her at the price of her silence.

CARTE, MRS. D'OYLY.—Maiden name, Miss Helen Cowper-Black. Educated at London University. Arranged lecture tours, including those of Archibald Forbes, Matthew Arnold, Serjeant Ballantine, and Oscar Wilde. Became Secretary and translator of the Opera Comique Company. After her marriage with Richard D'Oyly Carte she assisted him in the management of the Savoy Theatre, and, on his decease, took over the entire control until the close of her tenancy of the theatre in 1909, when, for a time, the operatic season was continued by the Savoyard, C. H. Workman.

CARTE, RICHARD D'OYLY.—Real name, Richard Doyle McCarthy. Son of one of the partners of Rudall, Carte & Co., the musical instrument makers, still in Berners Street. Like his wife, was educated at London University. Between 1871 and 1875 managed various productions, and arranged the farewell performances of the celebrated opera singer Mario. With the exception of the second and third sections of the original production of *Trial by Jury*, he was responsible for every Gilbert and Sullivan *première*. He built the Savoy Theatre, the Savoy Hotel, and the Palace Theatre, the last named being called the Royal English Opera House, and opening with Sullivan's *Ivanhoe*. Born May 3, 1844; died April 3, 1901.

CASILDA (G.).—Daughter of the Duke of Plaza-Toro and Queen of Barataria; in love with Luiz, who eventually turns out to be the King.

Castles.—The Castles mentioned in the operas are: Tremorden Castle, acquired by Major-General Stanley (Pir.); Castle Bunthorne (Pat.); Castle Hildebrand and Castle Adamant (P.I.); Ruddigore Castle (R); and Windsor Castle (implied), from whence Leonard Meryll brings a despatch (Y.).

"Cat was killed by care, Once a" (Pin. 2).—Derived from "Hang sorrow! Care will kill a cat," from George Wither's Poem on Christmas (*circa* 1623).

Catchy-Catchies ("Men are grown-up catchy-catchies." Pin. 2).—Either a term of endearment given to a baby when throwing him up in the air and catching him, or the name given by children in bygone times to the one who was "he" in a game of touch.

CATHCART, MAUD.—Appeared in the original production of *Iolanthe* both as Leila and Celia.

CAVE-ASHTON, MADAME.—Appeared in the original production of *The Sorcerer* as Aline.

CELIA (I.).—One of Strephon's fairy aunts, who subsequently allies herself to Earl Mountararat.

CELLIER, ALFRED.—Conductor of several of the earlier operas. A fellow chorister with Sullivan as a boy at the Chapel Royal. Made his fame as a composer with *Dorothy* in 1886. His last opera, *The Mountebanks*, was written in conjunction with Gilbert.

CELLIER, FRANÇOIS.—Brother of Alfred. He was the conductor of all the later operas, and remained with Mrs. D'Oyly Carte to the end.

Cervical ("his cervical vertebrae." M. 2).—Pertaining to the neck. The proper pronunciation is "serv-ȳ-cal," but for the purposes of the metre and the music, the "i" must be rendered short.

Chancery Lane ("A servile usher . . . led me, still singing, into Chancery Lane." I. 1).—This could not have happened at the present Law Courts, for they do not lead into Chancery Lane. But *Iolanthe* was produced a month before they were opened, and before then Chancery cases were sometimes heard in Lincoln's Inn Hall, or the old Rolls Court, Clifford's Inn, both of which lead into the Lane. Mentioned also in Pat. 2. "A Chancery Lane young man."

CHARD, KATE.—Created the part of Lady Psyche in *Princess Ida*.

C

CHARLES, MR.—Created the part of Sir Jasper Murgatroyd, the 3rd Baronet, in *Ruddigore*.

Chassepôt Rifle (Pir. 1).—A breech-loading, centre-firing gun, so-called from its inventor, a Frenchman named A. A. Chassepôt. In revivals this was changed to the more modern allusion "Mauser rifle."

Cherry Brandy (I. 2).—Mentioned in the Lord Chancellor's Song. The association of cherry brandy with pastrycooks is due to a practice in Victorian days, now no longer necessary. It was considered quite out of the question for gentlewomen to enter hotels or restaurant lounges. Consequently, high-class pastrycooks such as Hadden's in Gower Street and Luck's in Tottenham Court Road used to supply cherry brandy, which was often a substitute for afternoon tea.

"Chick that hatches, Only count the" (Pin. 2).—Suggested by the following lines in Samuel Butler's *Hudibras*:—

> "To swallow gudgeons ere they're catched
> And count their chickens ere they're hatched."

Children's *Pinafore*.—A series of matinées in 1879–80 played entirely by children, several of whom became well-known adult players. The cast included Emily Grattan, Ettie Mason, Louisa Gilbert, Harry Grattan, Harry Eversleigh, Edward Walsh, Edward Pickering, William Phillips, and Augustus Fitzclarence. The Grattans made a name later as comedy artists; Eversleigh, who died young, played in Willie Edouin's Company; while Pickering became acting manager at the Palace Theatre.

Children's *Pirates*.—A series of Savoy matinées in 1882 played entirely by children. The cast included Elsie Joel, Alice Vicat, Eva Warren, Florence Montrose, Georgie Esmond, Harry Tebbutt, Stephen Adeson, Edward Perry, William Pickering, and Charles Adeson. Most of the above became ornaments of the adult professional stage.

Chloe (P.I.).—One of the Girl Graduates. She loses three terms for making a sketch of a double perambulator, but, when war is declared, becomes Captain of the Fusiliers.

Chloe ("Come, Chloe and Phyllis." R. 1).—Typical name for a pastoral sweetheart. It occurs first in Longus's ode "Daphnis and Chloe," in the fourth century.

CHOLMONDELEY, SIR RICHARD (Y.).—Lieutenant of the Tower of London. The only character in the operas who was a real personage. He held office during the early part of Henry VIII's reign. His cenotaph and that of his wife, Lady Elizabeth, are in St. Peter ad Vincula. His effigy is recumbent and in mail armour, with collar and pendant. The Lieutenant is second in command, his superior officer being the Constable and the Resident Governor immediately under him. Pronounced Chumley.

Choregus ("The *choregus* of the early Attic stage." G.D. 2).—A chorus-master. Specifically, one who supervised the singing and dancing at the musical contests in Athens. Pronounced, "Kor-ēē-gus."

Choreutae ("The *choreutae* of that cultivated age."

37

G.D. 2).—Greek choral dancers. Pronounced "Kor-ēw-tee."

CHRISTO, MISS M.—Appeared in the original production of *Ruddigore* as Dame Hannah.

Chronos ("Oh, Chronos, Chronos, this is too bad of you." Pat. 1). (*Gr. Myth.*).—Time. Pronounced "Crón-noss."

Cimmerian Darkness ("The Cimmerian darkness of tangible despair." Pin. 1).—The Cimmerii were a race of people said to have lived almost in total darkness. They are first mentioned by Herodotus.

CITIZEN, FIRST (Y. 1).—The "unmannerly fellow" whom Elsie Maynard boxes on the ear for attempting to kiss her.

CITIZEN, SECOND (Y. 1).—The other unmannerly citizen who tries to kiss her after her performance and is threatened by her with a dagger.

CLARKE, HAMILTON.—Conductor of the third section of the original run of *Trial by Jury* and of subsequent operas. He is believed to have arranged several of the earlier Overtures.

CLARKE, JOHN S.—The celebrated comic actor, long associated with the Haymarket Theatre, who produced the third section of the original run of *Trial by Jury*.

Classical Monday Pops (M. 2).—Mentioned in the Mikado's Song. The classical popular concerts held at the old St. James's Hall, on the site of the present Piccadilly Hotel. The Ballads were held on Saturdays and the Classical Popular Concerts on Mon-

days. Also mentioned in Pat. 2: "Who thinks
suburban hops more fun than Monday Pops."

CLEARY, MINA.—Appeared in the original production of *The Gondoliers* as Gianetta.

"Cleave thee to the chine" (Y. 2).—Meaning "Split
thee to the backbone." This expression originates
from "I clove the rebel to the chine," from Otway's
play, *The Orphan*.

Clerical Characters.—The clerical characters in the
operas are: Dr. Daly (S.), Pooh-Bah (Archbishop
of Titipu) (M.), and the Ghost-Bishop who "is
never satisfied" (R.). In revivals, there was another,
the Chaplain who figures in the "execution scene"
(Y. 1).

CLIFTON, FRED.—Created the part of the Notary
in *The Sorcerer* and of Bill Bobstay in *Pinafore*.

"Climbing over rocky mountains" (Pir. 1).—This
chorus was taken, with altered words, from *Thespis*.

Coan Silk ("Their dress of Coan Silk was quite trans-
parent in design." G.D. 2).—Coa, famous for its
silk, was one of the islands of the Greek Archi-
pelago.

Cock and Bull ("Tell a tale of cock and bull." Y. 2).
—Various theories are extant concerning the
origin of this phrase. Some are fantastic, but the
generally accepted one is that it is handed down
from some fable where the animal and feathered
world talk like human beings. The French equivalent is *coq à l'ane*.

Coldharbour Tower (Y.).—Where Colonel Fairfax

is taken to spend his last hour with his confessor, and from whence he escapes. This tower once had a cell over it called the Nun's Bower, owing to its having been the prison of the Fair Maid of Kent.

COLE, ANNIE.—Created the part of Vittoria in *The Gondoliers*. Also appeared in the original production of *The Yeomen of the Guard* as Phoebe, and of *The Gondoliers* as Tessa.

Colfax, Richard (Y. 1).—One of Colonel Fairfax's fellow-prisoners in the Beauchamp Tower. See "Byfleet, Sir Martin."

Colocynth ("Something poetic lurks, even in colocynth." Pat. 1).—An Asiatic bitter gourd, resembling a water melon.

Common Pleas (I. 1).—Mentioned in the Lord Chancellor's Song. The Court of Common Pleas, instituted in the reign of Henry III, lasted until 1876, when it was incorporated in the Queen's (King's) Bench Division.

Conies ("I've chickens and conies." Pin. 1).—European wild rabbits.

CONNELL, E.—Appeared in the original production of *Trial by Jury* as the Counsel for the Plaintiff.

Constance (S.).—Mrs. Partlet's daughter, in love with the Vicar, Dr. Daly.

Contadine (G.) (*It.*).—Country girls. They are not necessarily flower-sellers.

Contango ("Which teaches what Contango means." U. 1).—In Stock Exchange parlance, interest paid to a seller to allow the buyer to postpone payment for stock until the next settling day. The antithesis to "Backwardation." (*q.v.*)

Contradicente ("Nobody at all *contradicente*." I. 1). (*Lat.*).—Contradicting. *Nemine contradicente*, often used when putting resolutions to the vote at meetings, means "nobody contradicting." If all vote the resolution is said to be "carried unanimously." Pronounced con-tra-dee-chén-tay.

CORCORAN, CAPTAIN (Pin.).—The Captain of H.M.S. *Pinafore*, and the father of Josephine.

CORCORAN, CAPTAIN SIR EDWARD, K.C.B. (U.).— One of the Six Flowers of Progress, representing the British Navy. Although he sings a portion of the "Captain of the *Pinafore*" Song, there is no reason to suppose that he is the same person, for Captain Corcoran was proved to be merely an A.B.

Cordova (G. 1).—The region where the husband of the King's foster-mother plied his trade as a brigand. It is on the Guadalquiver River. Pronounced "*Cór*-do-va."

Cornucopia ("Cornucopia is each in his mental fertility." U. 1).—The horn of plenty, represented with fruit and flowers emerging from it. The emblem of abundance. (*Rom. Myth.*)

Coronal ("Time weaves my coronal." P.I. 2).—A Spenserian word meaning a crown or garland.

Corybantian ("Corybantian mani*ac* kick." G.D. 2).— Corybant was a priest of Cybele in Phrygia who presided over rites which were accompanied with frenzied dancing. The usual adjective is "Corybantic." In the quotation, the last syllable of "maniac" is accented so that the finals may rhyme with "Bacchic."

COUNSEL FOR THE PLAINTIFF (T. by J.).—He appears for Angelina. The Defendant conducts his own case.

Court of St. James's Hall (U. 2).—This refers to the lower hall which for many years was occupied by the Moore and Burgess Minstrels. See "Classical Monday Pops." The scene which occurs when the above is mentioned is a burlesque of a meeting of the Privy Council.

Court of the Exchequer ("Is this the Court of the Exchequer?" T. by J.).—See "Exchequer."

COURTENAY, J.—Appeared in the original production of *Trial by Jury* as the Defendant.

Coutts ("The aristocrat who banks with Coutts." G. 1).—This famous London bank was absorbed by the National Provincial Bank in 1919.

COX, HARRY.—Appeared in the original production of *Trial by Jury* as the Usher.

COX, MR.—Created the part of the tenth baronet, Sir Mervyn Murgatroyd, in *Ruddigore*.

CRAVEN, HAWES.—Famous scenic artist, chiefly associated with the productions of Sir Henry Irving. He painted the scenery for Act II of *Princess Ida*.

Crichton ("A Crichton of early romance." R. 1).—

The original "Admirable Crichton" was a Scotsman named James Crichton, who, in the sixteenth century, took his M.A. degree at the age of fourteen.

CROSS, EMILY.—Created the part of Ruth in the original (London) production of *The Pirates of Penzance*.

Crown ("An hundred crowns." Y. 1).—The crown was first struck in the reign of Henry VIII, the period of the opera. It was then a gold piece of five shillings, worth about three times that amount in to-day's reckoning. Elsie's dowry, therefore, was about £75.

CUMMINGS, RICHARD.—Created the part of Go-To in *The Mikado*.

Cuneiform ("Babylonic cuneiform." Pir. 1).—Wedge-shaped, referring to the arrow-headed shape of the characters of Assyrian inscriptions.

CYRIL (P.I.).—One of Prince Hilarion's friends, who in a drunken song gives the Prince away. He subsequently weds Lady Pysche.

Cytharean posies (R. 1).—From Mad Margaret's Song. Flowers gathered in honour of Venus. From Cytheron (now Corigo), an Aegean island devoted to the worship of the goddess. (*Gr. Myth.*)

Czar ("Get at the wealth of the Czar if you can." Pat. 1).—From the Colonel's Song.

D

DAGMAR, CARLA.—Appeared in the original production of *The Grand Duke* as Julia Jellicoe.

DALY, DR. (S.).—Vicar of Ploverleigh. He is subsequently allied to Constance, the pew-opener's daughter.

Damme ("He said 'Damme.'" Pin. 2).—The only swear-word written in full in the operas, used by Captain Corcoran, and repeated with apparent gusto by the chorus. The Captain had previously admitted that he occasionally uses a "big, big D." Major-General Stanley (Pir. 2) uses the same word to the Sergeant of Police, but 'this is an interpolation, as is Wilfred Shadbolt's "Curse him" (Y. 1). So particular were Victorian playgoers, that even the wicked baronets of Ruddigore did not use bad language, and even Strephon's expression "a couple of confounded Radicals" (I. 1) was thought by some to be too strong. But the *fin de siècle* brought about a change, for in *Utopia Ltd.* the King actually twice says "Damn," though in the libretto it is judiciously indicated by "D——."

Daphnephoric ("With a Daphnephoric bound." Pat. 1).—"Laurel-bearing." The Daphnephoric revels at Thebes in honour of Apollo were preceded by a youth who leapt about bearing a sprig of laurel, one of the emblems of the god. (*Gr. Myth.*)

D'AUBAN, JOHN.—A famous London dancing master, who arranged the dances in most of the earlier operas.

Daughters of the Plough (P.I. 2).—The serving maids
at Castle Adamant. The Savoy collaborators' rule
concerning the impersonation of one sex by the
other has been broken in this opera, for these
"serving maids" are usually taken by male members
of the chorus, with long flaxen wigs.

DAUNTLESS, RICHARD (R.).—Robin Oakapple's foster-
brother, a man-o'-war's man. Thrown over by
Rose Maybud, he eventually finds consolation in
Zorah, the chief professional Bridesmaid.

Deadeye ("A better hand at turning a deadeye don't
walk a deck." R. 1).—A wooden block pierced
with three holes to receive a lanyard, used to
extend shrouds and stays. (*Naut.*)

DEADEYE, DICK (Pin.).—Able Seaman. Not very able,
however, for his right eye is blind and his left side
paralysed.

Decalet ("Here is a decalet," Pat. 2).—A ten-lined
verse, of which "Gentle Jane" and "Teasing Tom"
are correct examples.

Decapited ("Who's next to be decapited." M. 1).—
This is a Gilbertian word. The real one is "decapi-
tated."

DEFENDANT, THE (T. by J.).—He is sued for breach
of promise of marriage by the Plaintiff. See "Edwin
and Angelina."

Defoe, Daniel (Pat. 1).—Mentioned in the Colonel's
Song. The writer of *Robinson Crusoe* was a prolific
and versatile author, his best work, probably, being
his *Journal of the Plague Year*. He died in 1721.

Della Cruscan ("You are not Della Cruscan." Pat. 1).
—Applied to a school of aesthetic English writers
living mainly in Florence, about the year 1785.
Their methods were on the lines of the Accademia
della Crusca, founded in the sixteenth century for
the preservation of the pure Italian language.

DENNY, W. H.—Created the parts of Wilfred Shadbolt in *The Yeomen of the Guard*; Don Alhambra in
The Gondoliers; and Scaphio in *Utopia Ltd.*

DE PLEDGE, GEORGE.—Created the part of
Giorgio in *The Gondoliers*. Appeared in the original
production of *The Yeomen of the Guard* as Sir Richard
Cholmondeley.

Derring do ("Hail the valiant fellow who did this
deed of derring do." Y. 2).—An obsolete term
meaning a daring deed. It was used first by Spenser
in his *Faerie Queene:* "Drad for his derring doe."

Derry down derry (R. 2).—This old expression, used
merely as a convenient choral ejaculation in
madrigals, etc., really means "up and down" (the
scale). It is to be found as far back as in Udall's
Ralph Royster-Doyster, 1553.

De trop ("You're decidedly *de trop*." U. 1) (*Fr.*).—
Literally "too much." Usually meaning "nōt
wanted."

Devon ("Who started this morning from Devon."
I. 2).—From the Lord Chancellor's Song.

Dialect.—Gilbert makes very little use of dialect. Most
of the characters, of whatever social standing, speak
the purest English. Thus a boor like Wilfred Shad-

46

bolt is as refined in his speech as Colonel Fairfax. There are, however, a few exceptions. Dick Deadeye and Bill Bobstay occasionally speak with a nautical flavour (Pin.). Mrs. Partlet drops her "h's" (S.). Archibald Grosvenor at the end of Act II says "Oh, I sye!" (Pat.). Richard Dauntless's grammar is not always of the best (R.). Viscount Mentone (G.D.) talks Cockney, and Ben Hashbaz in the manner of an East End Yiddisher. But that is practically all.

Diergeticon ("Probably we shall, anon, sing a Diergeticon." G.D. 2).—This appears to be a coined word, used to impart atmosphere. It is not to be found in Liddell and Scott's *Lexicon*. There are, however, several Greek words from which it may be derived. Pronounced "Dy-eer-gét-i-kon," with a hard "g."

Differential Calculus ("I'm very good at integral and differential calculus." Pir. 1).—A method of investigating questions by using the ratio of indefinite small quantities called differentials. (*Math.*)

Dignified Clergy ("I has as lief not take post again with the dignified clergy." Y. 1).—This is not just a picturesque expression used by Jack Point, but a recognized term. The dignified clergy are the body of ecclesiastics occupying high office in the Church. The parish priests and curates are known as the undignified clergy.

Dimity ("Pray observe the magnanimity we display to lace and dimity." Pir. 1).—A cotton fabric, plain or frilled, used formerly for women's undergarments.

Dionysiac ("Dionysiac or Bacchic." G.D. 2).—Dionysos is the same as Bacchus, the god of wine. (*Gr. Myth.*)

Divines.—The divines mentioned in the operas are: Thomas Aquinas (Pat. 1); Archbishop of Canterbury (see Note under A) (Y. 1); Dr. Sacheverell (Pat. 1); and Dr. Watts (P.I. 1). Also a reference to some Bishop of Sodor and Man (Pat. 1).

Divining rods (S. 1).—These, which are used to discover water or metal underground, are the forked branches of the witch-hazel tree.

Divorce (I. 1).—Mentioned, in the sense of the Divorce Court, in the Lord Chancellor's Song. At the reorganization of the Courts, the Divorce Court was amalgamated with those of Probate and Admiralty.

Djinn ("Our resident Djinn." S. 1).—In Mohammedan mythology, an evil spirit. The word is actually the plural of "djinnee."

Doctors.—The only medical man mentioned in the operas is Sir James Paget (Pat. 1).

"Does your mother know you're ——" (I. 2).—This line is often lost upon the new generation. In Victorian and Edwardian days, "Does your mother know you're out" was a form of banter common with the lower classes.

"Dogs are found in many mangers" (Pin. 2).—The story of the Dog in the Manger is one of Aesop's Fables.

DOLARO, SELINA.—Although this popular opera-singer never played in Gilbert and Sullivan works, she shared with D'Oyly Carte the management of the first production of *Trial by Jury*. She had, indeed, intended to play the Plaintiff, but found that the lead in Offenbach's *La Perichole*, which was given on the same occasion, was enough for her, and the former part was allotted to Nellie Bromley. (*q.v.*)

Dolce far niente (I. 1; G. 1; U. 1) (*It.*).—The sweet state of doing nothing. Pronounced "dol-chay far nee-en-tay."

Doldrums ("Becalmed in the doldrums." R. 1).—A metaphor for a state of listlessness or inactivity. A part of the ocean, near the equator, so calm that navigation by sailing vessels may be held up for weeks.

DONALD, CARRIE.—Appeared in the original production of *The Gondoliers* as Gianetta.

"Don't say die" (I. 2).—From an old proverb, "Never say die; Up, man, and try."

D'Orsay ("The dash of a D'Orsay." Pat. 1).—From the Colonel's Song. Count D'Orsay, who shares with Beau Brummell the reputation of being the greatest dandy of the Regency, was an intimate friend of George IV when Prince Regent, and was a dashing and dissolute character.

Double-first ("Double-first in the world's university." U. 1).—A degree of the first class, both in classics and mathematics, at English universities.

Drachmae ("I'll pay them, if they back me, all in *oboloi* and *drachmae*." G.D. 2).—The Attic *drachma* was worth about 10d.

D

DRAKE, COLLARD.—One of the Directors of the Comedy Opera Company, who was a participator in the *Pinafore* riot.

DRAMALEIGH, LORD (U.).—A British Lord Chamberlain. One of the Flowers of Progress.

Drawing Room (U. 2).—The Drawing Room Scene, so far as ceremonial is concerned, is an exact portrayal of the British Court Drawing Room presentations. It is, in the opera, held in the evening, whereas in the Court of St. James's it always takes place in the afternoon, the evening ceremonial being the Levée at which gentlemen are presented. There were, however, certain interpolations in this scene of a burlesque character.

Drinks.—The following drinks are mentioned in the operas: barley water (R. 2); beef tea (R. 2); beer (Pat, 2; R. 1; G. 2; G.D. 2); brandy (G.D. 1); champagne (G.D. 2); cherry brandy (I. 2); coffee (Pin, 1; G. 2; U. 2); currant wine (G.D. 1); ginger-pop (U. 1; G.D. 1); Manzanilla (G. 2); Marsala (G.D. 2); Montero (G. 2); nectar (S. 1; M. 2; U. 1); Rhenish (G. 2); rum-punch (U. 1); sherry (Pir. 1; G. 2; U. 2); soda water (G.D. 1); tea (S.1; R. 2; U. 2; G.D. 1); toddy (G. 2).

"Drops the wind that stops the mill" (Pin. 2).—The original proverb, from Ray's Collection, is "No weather ill, if wind be still."

Dr. Watts's Hymns ("She'll scarcely suffer Dr. Watts's Hymns." P.I. 1).—Isaac Watts, the noted preacher, wrote many hymns, the best known being "O God, our help in ages past." Gilbert, who, except in this opera, seldom descends to puns, has here a play on the words "hymns" and "hims."

DUMMKOPF, ERNEST (G.D.).—A theatrical manager, who becomes technically dead after a statutory duel with Ludwig, his chief comedian. The word means a stupid-head.

DUNSTABLE, DUKE OF (Pat.).—Lieutenant in the 35th Dragoon Guards. He subsequently offers his hand to Lady Jane.

DWYER, MICHAEL.—Appeared in the original production of *Pinafore* as Captain Corcoran.

DYMOTT, MR.—Created the part of Bob Becket in *Pinafore*.

E

Early English ("You are not even Early English." Pat. 1).—The Early English period is reckoned from about 1150 to 1350.

Eastern Potentate ("An interesting Eastern potentate." G. 2).—This referred indirectly to the Shah of Persia, who had recently visited this country.

EASTON, FLORENCE.—Created the part of Phylla in *Utopia Ltd*.

Ecarté ("At middle-class party, I play at *ecarté*." G. 2). —A card game, of French origin, usually for two players. It consists largely of discarding cards, hence its name which means "discarded."

EDITH (Pir.).—One of Major-General Stanley's daughters. She becomes affianced to the Pirate King.

EDWARDS, MISS F.—Appeared in the original production of *Ruddigore* as Dame Hannah.

Edwin and Angelina (T. by J.).—The association of these two names has its origin in Oliver Goldsmith's *Hermit*.

EDWIN (T. by J.).—The Christian name of the Defendant, who is sued for breach of promise of marriage by the Plaintiff, Angelina.

"Eight years old" (Pir. 1).—This was the age at which Frederic was apprenticed to the Pirate King. It is thoroughly Gilbertian for an apprenticeship to last as long as thirteen years (if by years) or as short as $3\frac{1}{4}$ years (if by leap year birthdays).

Electuary ("— to buy an electuary for her." Y. 1).—

A common remedy in Tudor times. A medical powder done up as a sweet pill, which had to be *licked*, derived from the Greek ἐκλεικτον, a medicine that is licked away.

Elegiacs ("I quote in elegiacs." Pir. 1).—A set of verses in alternate hexameters and pentameters, the usual metre of the Latin poets, borrowed from the Greeks. In Y. 2, the four lines of the Chorus of Women commencing/"Comes the/pretty young /bride, : a-/blushing/timidly/shrinking//," called Elegiacs, are fine examples of this metre. The proper pronunciation is "Ell-e-gý-acs," with a hard "g."

Elision ("With greater precision, without the elision." R. 2).—This is capable of two explanations. (i) shortening of Sir Ruthven Murgatroyd to "Sir Murgatroyd." (ii) The pronunciation of Ruthven as it is spelt, instead of the more usual way "Rivven," adopted by the peer of that title. The second is the more likely explanation, partly because (ii) is of "greater precision" while (i) is not, and partly because a true elision is the contraction of a letter in a word, and not the elimination of a whole word.

ELLA, THE LADY (Pat.).—One of the Rapturous Maidens. She takes the soprano part in the Sextet, "I hear the soft note" in Act I.

Eloia (G.D. 2).—A fanciful expression of grief. It is not in the Greek Lexicon.

ELSA (G.D.).—One of the girls in Dummkopf's theatrical company.

Elysian ("What's the use of yearning for Elysian

fields?" Pat. 1).—The *'Ελύσιον πεδίον* of Greek mythology was the dwelling place of pure Souls after death. "Heavenly" is the modern equivalent. Also referred to in R. 1. ("The sudden transition is simply Elysian"), and in Pin. 2.

EMDEN, HENRY.—A well-known scenic artist, who painted the majority of the set-scenes of the operas. Thus, with Beverley and Hawes Craven, D'Oyly Carte secured for his productions the most famous scene-painters of the day.

Emetical ("Your placidity emetical." Pat. 2).—A polite way of saying "Sickening."

Emeutes ("When threatened with emeutes." Pir. 2).— An Anglicized French word meaning brawls or tumults. Pronounced "Emewts," its rhyme "boots" being usually rendered "bewts."

Empyrean ("towards the Empyrean heights." P.I. 2). —Pertaining to the highest and purest region of heaven. Pronounced "Em-py-rée-an."

"Enchantment must have been at work" (Y. 1).— All through the play, Dame Carruthers appears to be convinced that Fairfax's indictment as a sorcerer is a just one. She even calls him an "arch-fiend."

Epithalamia ("Let festive Epithalamia resound." G.D. 2) (*Lat.*).—An epithalamium was a nuptial song.

Equity draughtsman ("as an old equity draughts-man." I. 2).—Equity law is distinct from common law, but when the latter and the rules of equity are in conflict, equity law prevails.

Eros ("Oh, forgive her, Eros." Pat. 1).—The god of Love, the son of Aphrodite (*Gr. Myth.*). In Latin mythology, Cupid, the son of Venus. Strictly speaking, the word should be pronounced "Err-OSS," with a long "O," but in practice a short "O" is less pedantic. The "E" should always be short.

Etui ("Here is an *étui* dropped by one of them." P.I. 2) (*Fr.*).—A small case or purse used for scissors, needles, etc.

EVERARD, HELEN.—Created the parts of Mrs. Partlet in *The Sorcerer* and of Little Buttercup in *Pinafore*. Owing to illness, she did not create the part of Ruth in *The Pirates of Penzance* (London), but she played it later on several occasions.

"Every journey has an end" (I. 2).—This old proverb refers to a day's march, usually reckoned at twenty miles, which constituted a day's "journey." This association with labour and day (*jour*) is retained in the word "journeyman," a man hired to work by the day.

Exchequer ("Is this the Court of the Exchequer?" T. by J.).—The Court of Exchequer was abolished in 1876, and such cases as breach of promise transferred to the Queen's (King's) Bench. Also mentioned in Lord Chancellor's Song (I. 1).

"Experiments . . . are made on humble subjects" (P.I. 3).—The origin of this is "Fiat experimentum in corpore vilo." This saying arose out of the experience of one Muret, a French humorist (1526–1585), who, in a trance, narrowly escaped dissection at the hands of experimenting surgeons.

F

"Faint heart never won fair lady" (I. 2).—The proverb is found, in varying forms, in Britain's *Ida*; King's *Orpheus and Eurydice*; and Colman's *Love Laughs at Locksmiths*. But the best known is "Faint heart ne'er wan a lady fair," from Burns's *Epistle to Dr. Blacklock*.

FAIRFAX, COLONEL (Y.).—Under sentence of death for Sorcery. His Christian name is never divulged, and he is the only male character who wears three complete different costumes.

Fandango ("Dance a cachucha, fandango, bolero." G. 2).—A Spanish dance in 6/8 time. It is slow, and akin to the seguidillas, and danced by two persons using castanets.

FARREN, NELLY.—The famous Gaiety Theatre favourite, who played Mercury in *Thespis*. She was the sole example, in Gilbert and Sullivan works, of a woman playing a male part, or *vice versa*. The nearest approach to a breach of this rule is the case of Hilarion, Cyril, and Florian (P.I.), but they only *pretend* to be women until circumstantial danger makes them act the parts in earnest. The playing of the Midshipmite (Pin.) by a girl was not sanctioned by Gilbert and Sullivan. However, in later productions of *Princess Ida*, the parts of the "Daughters of the Plough" (in order to preserve the correct number of the Girl Graduates) have been taken by male members of the chorus.

FERRIS, D'ARCY.—Appeared in the original production of *Pinafore* as Ralph Rackstraw. He was the father of Joan de Ferrers, the operatic soprano.

Festina lente ("as the ancient Romans said, *Festina lente*." I. 1).—Best rendered colloquially as "Go slow!" This Latin saying forms the punning motto of the family of Onslow.

FIAMETTA (G.).—One of the Contadine. She sings the first solo in the opera.

Fico ("A fico for such boons, say we!" U. 2).—A fig (*It.*).—An insignificant trifle. The expression occurs in Shakespeare.

Fiddle-de-dee (R. 2).—This expression is first used by Dr. Johnson.

Fielding ("The humour of Fielding, which sounds contradictory." Pat. 1).—From the Colonel's Song. Henry Fielding, author of *Tom Jones* and *Joseph Andrews*. The "contradictory" aspect is that, in cricket, there is not supposed to be much fun in fielding.

FINDLAY, JOSEPHINE.—Created the part of Zorah in *Ruddigore*. Also appeared in the original production as Rose Maybud, and in that of *The Mikado* as Yum-Yum.

FIRST BRIDESMAID (T. by J.).—She stands on the extreme O.P. side and receives a *billet-doux* from the Judge, which later is transferred, at his instruction, to the Plaintiff.

Fish.—The fish mentioned in the operas are: brill

(Pin. 2); goldfish (I. 1); herring (Y. 2); salmon (I. 1); shrimp (Pat. 2); and turbot (Pin. 2).

Fish in the sea (i. "There's lots of good fish in the sea." M. 1; ii. "There's fish in the sea . . . as good as ever came out of it." Pat. 1).—The original proverb is "Be content, the sea hath fish enough."

FISHE, SCOTT.—Created the part of Mr. Goldbury in *Utopia Ltd.*; and of the Prince of Monte Carlo in *The Grand Duke*. He appeared later in revivals of most of the operas, and met with a sad and tragic end.

FISHER, WALTER.—Created the part of the Defendant in *Trial by Jury*.

FITZBATTLEAXE, CAPT. (U.).—Of the First Life Guards, and betrothed to Princess Zara. His Christian name is Arthur.

"Five and a little bit over" (Pir. 2).—The computed age of Frederic, reckoning by birthdays. See "1940."

FLEET, DUNCAN.—Appeared in the original production of *The Gondoliers* as Giuseppe.

FLETA (I.).—One of the three principal Fairy Aunts of Strephon.

FLORIAN (P.I.).—One of Hilarion's friends, and the brother of Lady Psyche. He subsequently weds Melissa.

Flowers and Plants.—The flowers and plants mentioned in the operas are: asphodel (Pat. 1; P.I. 2); buttercup (I. 1; P.I. 2); cactus (P.I. 2); daisy

(Pir. 1; Pin. 1); deadly nightshade (R. 2); heather (U. 2); hollyhock (P.I. 2); lily (Pat. 1; R. 1); poppy (Pat. 1); rose (T. by J.; P.I. 2; R. 1; G. 1; U. 1); stinging nettle (P.I. 2); sunflower (S. 2; P.I. 2); tulip (Pat. 2); and violet (P.I.; R. 1; G.D. 2).

Food.—The following forms of food are mentioned in the operas: apple-puff (I. 2); Banbury cakes (I. 2); beef (T. by J.); biscuits (U. 2); bread (P.I. 1; G. 2; G.D. 1); bun (S. 1; G. 2); butter (Pat. 1); cheese (G. 2; G.D. 1); chickens (Pin. 1); chops (Pin. 1; Pat. 2); conies (Pin. 1); eggs (S. 1; G.D. 1); gravy (Pat. 1); ham (S.1); ices (G. 2); lamb (P.I. 2); macaroni (G. 2); mock turtle soup (G.D. 1); muffins (S. 1); mutton (T. by J.); plum jam (Pat. 2); polonies (Pin. 1); roly-poly pudding (Pat. 2); rusk (G. 2); Sally Lunn (S. 1); sandwich (G.D. 2); sausage (Y. 2); sausage roll (G.D. 1); three-cornered tarts (I. 2); toast (S. 1); treacle (Pin. 1).

Forehead ("It wasn't written on his forehead." M. 2). —This is always pronounced as written, and not in the colloquial way of "forrid." A similar idea to this line is conveyed by Shadbolt in Y. 2 concerning the word "brother" not being written on Leonard's brow.

FOREMAN OF THE JURY (T. by J.).—He sits in the jury box nearest to the Judge, and makes love to the Plaintiff before she is invited up to the Bench.

Foreyard arm (Pin. 1).—A foreyard is the lowest yard on the foremast. (*Naut.*)

F

Forsooth (Y. 1).—This expression, meaning "in truth," is of Anglo-Saxon origin, "sooth" being the equivalent for "truth."

FORSTER, KATE.—Appeared in the original performance of *The Gondoliers* as the Duchess of Plaza-Toro. She was for many years the principal "grande dame" of the touring company.

FORTESCUE, MABEL.—Created the part of Celia in *Iolanthe*. Later she was the leading figure in a famous breach of promise case, in which she invoked general sympathy and which she won.

Foster-brother.—The foster-brothers in the operas are Captain Corcoran and Ralph Rackstraw (presumably) (Pin.); Richard Dauntless and Robin Oakapple (R.); Colonel Fairfax and Leonard Meryll (Y.); and Luiz and one of the Palmieris (G.).

Fra Angelican ("How Fra Angelican. Pat. 2).—In the style of Michelangelo, the great Italian painter and sculptor, 1475–1564. Fra, meaning brother, was applied to lay brothers and secular priests. Italian painters used to belong to secular orders, so that they were permitted to adorn sacred edifices.

Francesca di Rimini (Pat. 2).—The heroine of Dante's story in his *Inferno*. She fell in love with her prospective brother-in-law Paolo, and both were slain by her husband-elect.

FRANCESCO (G.).—One of the Gondoliers, the part being taken by a tenor.

FREDERIC (Pir.).—The pirate apprentice, in love with Major-General Stanley's daughter, Mabel.

French.—A word Gilbert uses to express something *risqué*. It occurs twice: (i) "A not too French French bean" (Pat. 1). (ii) "A joke that's too French" (Y. 2).

French bean.—In using the expression "A not too French French bean," Gilbert was, perhaps unconsciously, stating a fact. A French bean has nothing to do with France; it comes from South America.

Fruit and Vegetables.—The fruit and vegetables mentioned in the operas are: apple (R. 1; Y. 1); asparagus (G. 2); cauliflower (I. 2); cocoanut (U. 2); cranberries (I. 2); cucumber (P.I. 2); French bean (Pin. 1); grapes (I. 2); mustard and cress (S. 1); nut (Y. 2); peaches (R. 1; G. 2); peas (I. 2; R. 1); pickles (I. 2); pineapple (I. 2); potato (Pin. 1); raisins (Y. 2; G.D. 1).

Full Court ("It could be argued, six months hence, before the full court." M. 1). See " In banc."

Furbelow ("frill and furbelow." P.I. 1).—This word, meaning a plaited flounce, is derived from the Provincial French word "farbala."

G

Gaddersby, Gaffer (R. 1).—One of the objects of Rose Maybud's charity. Gaffer is a colloquialism for "grandfather."

Garnet, Sir ("Skill of Sir Garnet in thrashing a cannibal." Pat. 1).—From the Colonel's Song. Sir Garnet Wolseley was Commander-in-Chief of the British Army (1895–1900), and died in 1913. By a curious coincidence, he was created a peer, Viscount Wolseley, on the day of the last performance of the original production of *Patience*.

Gask ("(Let) Gask (secede) from Gask." P.I. 2).— A celebrated firm of silk mercers of Oxford Street.

George (I. 2).—The Christian name of the Earl of Mountararat.

Gerard Dow ("I can tell undoubted Raphaels from Gerard Dows. . . ." Pir. 1).—Gerhard Dow (1613–1680) was a pupil of Rembrandt. His "Poulterer's Shop" and his auto-portrait are in the National Gallery.

Gerolstein ("It's a very good part in Gerolstein." G.D. 1).—Referring to Offenbach's *Grand Duchess of Gerolstein*. This work was put on at the Savoy Theatre, for the first and last time, a few months after *The Grand Duke* was withdrawn, the cast including Florence St. John, Walter Passmore, and Henry Lytton.

Giacopo (G. 2).—The old boatman who conveyed Gianetta and Tessa to the island of Barataria. The correct way to pronounce it is "Já-co-po." See "Gianetta."

GIANETTA (G.).—One of the two principal Contadine, married to Marco. The correct pronunciation is of the utmost importance. It is a trisyllabic word, and is used by both Gilbert and Sullivan as such. The "i" is not a separate vowel and does not constitute a syllable, but is used merely to soften the "g" and make it sound like the French "j." The name, therefore, should be pronounced "Janetta," not "Gee-a-net-ta." This treatment of "Gi" applies also to Giacopo, Giorgio, Giulia, and Giuseppe.

Gideon Crawle (R. 2).—This ejaculation made by Sir Ruthven to Old Adam is apparently incomprehensible. But its solution may be that (as Robin Oakapple was Sir Ruthven's assumed name), so Old Adam was originally intended to be merely the assumed name of his faithful servant, whose real name was Gideon Crawle. Another possible solution is that it was a character in some contemporary melodrama of the kind which Gilbert was satirizing in this opera.

Gillow's ("Everything that isn't old, from Gillow's." Pin. 2).—It was many years after the production of *Pinafore* that this firm, noted for its elegant modern furniture and bric-à-brac, was amalgamated with Waring's.

GILBERT, CHARLES.—Appeared in the original production of *The Yeomen of the Guard* as Sir Richard Cholmondeley and Wilfred Shadbolt.

GILBERT, SIR WILLIAM SCHWENK.—Born in Southampton Street, Strand, November 18, 1836.

Educated at London University. Was a clerk in the Privy Council Office, 1857–1862; called to the Bar in 1864; married the daughter of Captain Turner, 1867; was a Captain in the Royal Aberdeen Militia in 1868; later was made J.P. and Deputy-Lieutenant of the County of Middlesex; was Knighted in 1907. His first theatrical work was the burlesque *Dulcamara* (1866), and his last a melo-dramatic sketch *The Hooligans*, written for the late James Welch (1911). He died on May 29, 1911, in a gallant endeavour to save a young girl visitor at his home, Grim's Dyke, who had got into difficulties in the bathing pool.

Gilded dukes (S. 1).—The adjective "gilded" is asso-ciated with the peerage, probably due to eligibility to membership of the House of Lords—the "gilded chamber." Captain Corcoran (S. 1) also refers to "some gilded lordling."

Gioco ("Would distinctly be no *gioco*." M. 1).—There is no such word, meaning "joke." The nearest Italian approach is *giocolo* or *giuoco*.

Giorgio (G.).—One of the Gondoliers. See "Gian-etta."

Girton ("At Girton, all is wheat." U. 1).—The Women's College at Cambridge where Princess Zara received her English education.

Giulia (G.).—One of the Contadine. See "Gianetta."

Giuseppe (G.).—One of the principal Gondoliers, married to Tessa. The reputed brother of Marco. See "Gianetta."

GOLDBURY, MR. (U.).—A Company Promoter. One of the Six Flowers of Progress, representing Finance.

GONDOLIERS, THE, or *THE KING OF BARATARIA.* —The eleventh opera. Produced at the Savoy Theatre, December 7, 1889. It ran till June 20, 1891, the total performances being 559. Revived in 1898 (twice), 1907, and 1909, the total aggregate performances being 782.

NOTES ON "THE GONDOLIERS"

The chief newcomers were Frank Wyatt, who with his wife Violet Melnotte became proprietors of the Trafalgar Square Theatre (now the Duke of York's Theatre); and Decima Moore, tenth child of the Public Analyst of Brighton, sister of Bertha, Jessie, and Eva Moore, and, later, Lady Guggisberg.

———

Cissie Saumarez, who later became Mrs. Arthur Whitby, created a record in this production. She played, at one time or another, no fewer than six characters: Gianetta, Tessa, Casilda, Fiametta, Vittoria, and Giulia.

———

Another record was made in the number of ladies who appeared as Gianetta. They were fifteen in number, and included: Geraldine Ulmar, Leonore Snyder, Cissie Saumarez, Emily Squire, Carrie Donald, Annie Schuberth, N. Phyllis, Amy Sherwin, Alice Baldwin, Mina Cleary, Maude Holland, Louise Pemberton, Esther Palliser, Miss Carritte, and Nellie Lawrence.

At first there was a ballad for Luiz in Act I,
the words being:

"With mocking smile
    My love beguile;
With idle jest
    Appease my breast;
With angry voice
    My soul rejoice;
Beguile with scorn
    My heart forlorn!
O happy he, who is content to gain
Thy scorn, thy angry frown, thy deep
    disdain."

But this was cut out in order to give more vocal
work to Decima Moore, and the now familiar
"There was a time" substituted.

During the long run of a year and a half, perfect
attendances were made by Annie Bernard, W.
Medcalf, and G. de Pledge.

On March 6, 1891, the first and only command
performance of any of the operas was given at
Windsor Castle. It took place in the Waterloo
Chamber, and there was a full cast. François
Cellier conducted; W. H. Seymour was stage
manager; J. W. Beckwith, acting manager; and
D'Oyly Carte was present. The ladies' dressing-
room was the Throne Room, while the men were
accommodated in St. George's Hall. The audience
included Her Majesty Queen Victoria, the Empress
Frederick, and many others of the Royal Family.

GOODHEART, OLD ADAM (R.).—Robin Oakapple's
faithful servant.

Good Queen Bess ("In good Queen Bess's time." I. 2). From the Earl of Mountararat's Song. Queen Elizabeth and Queen Victoria ("In Queen Victoria's name," Pir. 2), and Queen Anne ("the reign of good Queen Anne," Pat. 1) are the only English Queens mentioned in the operas.

"Goose becomes a swan, Every" (G. 1).—This expression is very ancient. Thus it is found in Bishop Mountagu's "Gag": "With Catholikes every Pismire is a Potentate; and every Goose a Swan."

GORDON, DOUGLAS.—Appeared as Josephine in the original production of *Pinafore*.

Go-To (M.).—A Japanese noble lord. A character introduced to take the bass part in the Madrigal when the player of Pish-Tush was not vocally suitable. To him also is allotted the line in Act I, "Why, who are you who asks this question?"

Grandee (G.).—The highest rank in the Spanish nobility, a member of which is permitted to wear his hat in the presence of royalty. For the apparent discrepancy with regard to the Duke of Plaza-Toro's real rank, see "Hidalgo."

GRAND DUKE, THE, or *THE STATUTORY DUEL.* —The thirteenth and final opera. Produced at the Savoy Theatre, March 7, 1896, and ran till July 10, 1896, the total performances being 123. It was never revived.

NOTES ON "THE GRAND DUKE"

The most novel feature of the opera was a Hungarian lady speaking in broken English, representing an English girl speaking in broken German. The rest of the cast, speaking perfect English, were supposed to be speaking perfect German. The illusion was well maintained.

———

The Hungarian lady, Ilka von Palmay, was in private life the Countess von Kinsky.

———

The opera saw the first appearance of two artists destined to become famous. One was C. Herbert Workman, who had a few lines to say as the Jewish costumier. The other, who played the small part of Gretchen, was Ruth Vincent.

———

The Herald's Song is akin to the one in *Lohengrin*, and the Greek Procession scene is Wagnerian in character.

———

The Sausage Roll Song, which was considered by the critics to be a poor form of wit, has its justification in the popularity of the sausage in Germany, thereby making it a not unsuitable emblem for a German Secret Society.

———

Rudolph's reference to a Wedding March he had composed was a sly dig at the (ex-)Kaiser Wilhelm II, who had recently done a similar thing.

———

Lovers of coincidence may be interested to note that the first bars of the first opera *Trial by Jury* are in the same key (E major) as the last bars of the last opera, *The Grand Duke*.

GRAY, WARWICK.—Created the part of Guron in

Princess Ida. Also appeared in the original production of *Iolanthe* as Private Willis.

GRETCHEN (G.D.).—One of Ernest Dummkopf's theatrical company.

GREY, SYBIL.—Created the parts of Fleta in *Iolanthe*; of Sacharissa in *Princess Ida*; and of Peep-Bo in *The Mikado.* Appeared also in the original production of *The Pirates of Penzance* as Kate; of *Iolanthe* as Lady Saphir; and of *The Mikado* as Pitti-Sing.

GRIDLEY, LAWRENCE.—Created the part of Sir Edward Corcoran in *Utopia Ltd.*

Grig ("As merry as a grig." G.D. 1).—A grig may be a cricket, or a small eel, but the former is the one connected with this expression, which is often rendered "As merry as a cricket." It is thought to be a corruption of "As merry as a Greek."

GROSSMITH, GEORGE.—Created the parts of John Wellington Wells in *The Sorcerer*; Sir Joseph Porter in *Pinafore*; Major-General Stanley in *The Pirates of Penzance*; Reginald Bunthorne in *Patience*; the Lord Chancellor in *Iolanthe*; King Gama in *Princess Ida*; Ko-Ko in *The Mikado*; Robin Oakapple in *Ruddigore*; and Jack Point in *The Yeomen of the Guard.* (See Notes to *Trial by Jury.*)

GROSVENOR, ARCHIBALD (Pat.).—An idyllic poet, in love with Patience. See "Algernon."

Grosvenor Gallery ("A greenery-yallery, Grosvenor Gallery . . . young man." Pat. 2).—The New Grosvenor Gallery was opened in New Bond Street for the occupation of the Pre-Raphaelites, devotees of aesthetic art. Its members included Burne-Jones, Whistler, Swinburne, Holman Hunt, William Morris, and Oscar Wilde. Primarily for art exhibitions, it embraced all kinds of aestheticism. Later, the Art Section moved to the New Gallery.

Guizot (Pat. 1).—Mentioned in the Colonel's Song. The French statesman and author who became Premier. His policy led to the Revolution of 1848. He died in 1874.

Gurneys ("as rich as the Gurneys." T. by J.).—A Quaker family of Norwich bankers. The London branch, known as Overend, Gurney & Co., failed in 1866 with liabilities of over eleven million pounds. The Norwich branch was acquired by Barclays Bank in 1896.

Guron (P.I.).—One of Gama's three sons.

GWYNNE, JULIA.—Created the parts of Edith in *The Pirates of Penzance*; Lady Saphir in *Patience*; and Leila in *Iolanthe*. Also appeared in the original production of *Patience* as Lady Angela. Later became Mrs. George Edwardes.

H

Halbert ("Here is your halbert, Sir." Y. 1).—The halbert, or halberd, is a long-handled weapon of which the head has several sharp edges, as well as a curved or straight point. The heads were sometimes very elaborate.

Halfpennies ("dropped hot halfpennies down their backs." Pat. 2).—This word is always pronounced here as spelt.

Hamlet ("Flavour of Hamlet." Pat. 1).—From the Colonel's Song.

Handspike ("A keener hand . . . never shipped a handspike." Pir. 1).—A lever, generally of wood, for heaving anchor, in a windlass or capstan. (*Naut.*)

HANNAH, DAME (R.).—Rose Maybud's Aunt, self-condemned to an eternal spinsterhood, owing to her lover, Sir Roderic Murgatroyd, being a bad Baronet of Ruddigore. Her name is Miss Trusty.

Hannibal ("The genius strategic of . . . Hannibal." Pat. 1).—From the Colonel's Song. The great Carthaginian soldier who overthrew the Romans at Cannae in 216 B.C.

HARFORD, W.—Painted the scenery for the original production of *Pinafore* and of *The Grand Duke*.

Harwich ("tossing about in a steamer from Harwich." I. 2).—From the Lord Chancellor's Song. A famous port on the Essex coast.

H

HASWELL, BOWDEN.—Created the part of Calynx in *Utopia Ltd.*

HAVERS, MRS. ALICE.—The designer of the illuminated programmes in use at the Savoy Theatre. The first was used at the production of *Princess Ida* in 1884, and the last at the command performance of *The Gondoliers* at Windsor Castle in 1891.

HEADSMAN, THE (Y. 1).—He remains standing at the block until the final tableau of Act I. The axe blade is turned outwards when carried in procession, to denote that the prisoner is to be executed.

HEATHCOTE, MISS.—Created the part of Chloe in *Princess Ida.*

HEBE (Pin.).—Sir Joseph Porter's cousin, to whom he is finally allied.

Helen of Troy ("The seven thousand and thirty-seventh in direct descent from Helen of Troy." S. 1).—The absurdity of this claim is heightened by the fact that the date of the legendary Trojan War has never definitely been determined. The most that is known positively is that Aeschylus's tragedy of *Agamemnon* was performed in 458 B.C.

Helicon ("If you'd climb the Helicon." P.I. 2).—A mountain in Greece, where the Muses were supposed to dwell. (*Gr. Myth.*) Wrongly given in the Chatto and Windus edition as "*cross* the Helicon."

Heliogabalian ("One of the most Heliogabalian profligates." U. 1).—After the manner of Heliogabalus (*q.v.*).

Heliogabalus ("all the crimes of Heliogabalus." Pir. 1).—The most dissolute of all the Roman Emperors, he reigned from A.D. 220. His offences against morality were notorious, and he ended his life by being slain by the Pretorian Guards who protected the cousin he was endeavouring to have murdered. He reigned under the name of Marcus Aurelius Antoninus.

HENRI, H.—The name under which (Sir) Henry Lytton made his first appearance at the Savoy Theatre, when deputizing for Grossmith in *Ruddigore* in 1887. One of his reasons for taking this name was to pose, owing to his youth, as the brother of his wife (Lady Lytton), who was known' as Louie Henri. She herself appeared in a revival of *The Gondoliers* at the Savoy as Tessa.

HERALD (G.D.).—He announces in song the approach of the Prince of Monte Carlo.

HERCULES (S.).—The small page who ushers in John Wellington Wells from the tent where he has been taking refreshment.

HERVEY, ROSE.—Created the part of Kate in *The Yeomen of the Guard*. Also appeared in the original production of *Iolanthe* as Leila; of *Ruddigore* as Rose Maybud; and of *The Yeomen of the Guard* as Elsie Maynard.

Hessians ("A lover's professions, when uttered in Hessians." Pat. 1).—Boots invented in the German state Hesse, and adopted generally by army officers in the early part of the nineteenth century. They were top boots with ornamental tassels.

H

HEWSON, JONES.—Created the part of the Herald in *The Grand Duke*. Like Scott Fishe, he suffered from a delicate chest, and died young.

Hidalgo ("A Castilian hidalgo of ninety-five quarterings." G. 1).—The lowest order of Spanish nobility. The Duke of Plaza-Toro was, however, a Grandee, which is the highest order. See "Grandee."

Highlows ("Highlows pass as patent leathers." Pin. 2). —This appears to be a proverb originated by Gilbert. Highlows are laced boots, ankle high.

HILARION (P.I.).—King Hildebrand's son, betrothed to Princess Ida when he was two years old, and she one year.

Hipparchus ("Hipparchus 'twas, B.C. one-sixty-three." P.I. 2).—Celebrated Greek astronomer. 163 B.C. is probably a little too early a date as his mature activities dated from about 146 B.C. to 126 B.C.

"Hoity, toity" ("Sing, hoity, toity." P.I. 2).—This expression, used as an ejaculation of contempt, is first to be found in Congreve's comedy *Love for Love*.

HOLLAND, FANNY.—Appeared in the original production of *Pinafore* as Josephine. Whereas Leonora Braham came to the Savoy from the German Reed's Entertainment at St. George's Hall, Miss Holland left the D'Oyly Carte Company to become for many years a principal with the German Reeds.

HOLLAND, MAUDE.—Appeared in the original production of *The Gondoliers* as Gianetta.

HOLLINGSHEAD, JOHN.—The famous manager

of the Gaiety Theatre, under whose control *Thespis* was produced.

HOLLINGSWORTH, MR.—Created the part of Counsel for the Plaintiff in *Trial by Jury*.

HOOD, MARION.—Created the part of Mabel in *The Pirates of Penzance* (London). She subsequently became a Gaiety Theatre "star."

HOOPER, MISS M.—Appeared in the original production of *Iolanthe* as Celia.

Horace ("From Ovid and Horace." R. 1).—Quintus Horatius Flaccus, the famous Augustinian poet. He and Ovid were practically contemporaries.

Hornpipe ("Can you dance a hornpipe?" Pin. 1; "His hornpipe is the talk of the fleet." R. 1).—This sailor's dance is so-called because it is accompanied by a pipe or penny whistle. It is mentioned as early as the sixteenth century, by Sir Walter Raleigh.

Hour of ten ("Hark, the hour of ten is sounding." T. by J.).—The first words of the opera. High Court cases usually start at 10.30, but jurymen are often summoned for ten o'clock.

Howell and James ("A Howell and James young man." Pat. 2).—A famous firm of drapers, of Regent Street.

Hubble-bubble, Hurly-burly ("With a hurly-burly and a hubble-bubble." G.D. 2).—This is a Gilbertian extension of the expression "hub-bub," meaning a commotion. "Hubble-bubble" is the Oriental pipe known as a hookah, which, through being smoked through water, makes a bubbling noise. It is used

H

in Hood and Sullivan's *Rose of Persia*: "Hurly-burly," with a similar meaning to "hub-bub," is derived from the Old English word "hurly," confusion, and is allied to the French *hurler*, to howl.

Humanities (P.I.).—Of which Lady Psyche is the Professor. Those branches of learning which comprise the study of languages, classics, rhetoric, etc., as distinguished from religious science, known as Divinities.

Hungary ("Oh, doughty sons of Hungary." P.I. 3).—From this phrase, applied to Arac, Scynthius and Guron, we may gather that King Gama's nationality was Hungarian.

HUNT, MR.—Appeared in the original production of *Utopia Ltd.* as Tarara.

Hurdy-gurds ("grinning herds of hurdy-gurds." P.I. 3).—Poetical phrase for players of the hurdy-gurdy. This instrument is often considered synonymous with "barrel-organ." But it resembled more a piano-organ. It was boat-shaped, the strings being stopped by an apparatus of keys mounted over the soundboard and set in vibration by the friction of a wooden wheel charged with resin and turned by means of a handle.

Hyporchematic ("We've a choir hyporchematic." G.D. 2).—A hyporchema was a choral hymn to Apollo, accompanied with dancing and fantastic pantomime.

Hypotenuse ("With many cheerful facts about the square of the hypotenuse." Pir. 1).—The side of a right-angled triangle that is opposite the right angle. (*Trig.*)

76

I

IDA, PRINCESS (P.I.).—King Gama's daughter, the
Head of the Women's University at Castle Adamant,
betrothed in infancy to Prince Hilarion.

Idyl ("And 'High diddle diddle' will rank as an idyl."
Pat. 2).—A short pastoral poem, so-called first by
Ausonius. Strictly speaking, the initial I should be
long, as is the case with both the Latin and the
Greek terms. But it is often, as in this case, given
as a short I. Often spelt "idyll."

Illustrated Programmes.—See "Mrs. Alice Havers."

Implication, Inference, Innuendo ("by implication, by
inference, and by innuendo." Y. 1).—There is a
slight difference in the meaning of these terms. An
implication is that which is suggested but not
expressed; an inference that which may be fairly
deduced but not actually named; an innuendo is
an equivocal allusion, or something with a double
meaning, of an uncomplimentary or indelicate
nature.

In Banc ("Never be reversed *in Banc*." T. by J.).—In
full Court. The judgment of a High Court Judge is
liable to be reversed on appeal to the full Court,
in the first instance the Court of Appeal, and later
the appeal may be taken to the House of Lords.

INEZ (G.).—The Prince of Barataria's foster-mother.
At the time she was the wife of Baptisto Palmieri.

"In for a penny, in for a pound" (I. 2).—This proverb
is taken from a Spanish saying, "Preso per uno,

preso per cento" ("Imprisoned for one, imprisoned for a hundred"). The word "in" therefore signifies "in prison." Another proverb bearing the same idea is "One may as well be hanged for a sheep as for a lamb."

Insects and reptiles.—The following are the insects and reptiles mentioned in the operas: bee (I. 1; R. 1); blackbeetle (Y. 2; G.D. 1); bluebottle (Pat. 2; M. 2); cockatrice (Y. 2); earthworm (R. 2); flea (G. 2); fly (I. 2; R. 1); frog (I. 1; Pin. 2; G.D. 1); ladybird (R. 1); maggot (R. 2; Y. 2); spider (G.D. 1); tadpole (R. 2); toad (S. 1); turtle (G.D. 1); weevil (R. 2); and worm (R. 2).

Integral Calculus ("I'm very good at integral . . . calculus." Pir. 1).—The opposite to differential calculus (*q.v.*), meaning to learn from a known ratio of two or more magnitudes the relation of the magnitudes themselves. (*Math.*)

Intramural ("From charms intramural." R. 1).—Literally, "between walls." Here it is used in the sense of "town life."

IOLANTHE (I.).—Strephon's fairy mother who was banished by the Queen of the Fairies for marrying the mortal Lord Chancellor.

IOLANTHE, or *THE PEER AND THE PERI.*—The sixth opera. Produced at the Savoy Theatre, November 25, 1882. It ran till January 1, 1884, with a total of 400 performances. It was revived in 1901, 1907, and 1908, with an aggregate number of performances, 593.

The chief newcomer at the original production was Charles Manners, later the husband of Fanny Moody, and the director of the Moody-Manners Opera Company.

———

The original title selected was "Perola," to preserve the continuity of operas commencing with the letter "P" which had been so fortunate in the case of *Pinafore*, *Pirates*, and *Patience*.

———

This was the last opera in which Miss Fortescue appeared, but she was seen later in a work by Gilbert, playing at the Court Theatre in his play *Dan'l Druce*.

———

During this production the "queue" system was first introduced, at the Savoy Theatre, to the London stage. See "Queue."

———

It was the first opera to have its *première* at the Savoy Theatre.

Ipso facto.—Gilbert twice uses this Latin phrase, meaning "By the fact itself," once in G. 2 ("He will, *ipso facto*, boil down to a single gentleman"), and in G.D. 1 ("The dead man, *ipso facto*, will come to life again").

"I quite forget their name" (P.I. 3).—The leg-armour, the name of which Arac forgets, is called either jambes or greaves.

Isabel (Pir.).—One of Major-General Stanley's daughters.

79

I

"Is life a boon?" (Y. 1).—The beautiful stanza beginning with these words, which is a quotation from
the song sung by Colonel Fairfax just before his
expected execution, forms the inscription on the
Sullivan Memorial on Victoria Embankment.

J

"Jackdaws strut in peacock's feathers" (Pin. 2).—
From the Fable of the Jackdaw in *Aesop's Fables*.

Jacky ("Excellent jacky." Pin. 1).—Soft bread, generally in the form of new rolls.

JAMES (Pir.).—A pirate character included in the
original cast at the Paignton production. It was
played by John Le Hay. It was cut out of the
London production. The part was of no value
except to provide a suitor to the third principal
sister of Mabel, Isabel.

JANE, THE LADY (Pat.).—An elderly Rapturous
Maiden who persistently follows Bunthorne, but
eventually accepts the Duke of Dunstable.

JELLICOE, JULIA (G.D.).—An English comedienne,
playing lead in Ernest Dummkopf's Company, who,
after becoming the Grand Duchess for awhile,
returns to that manager.

JENOURE, AIDA.—Appeared in the original production of *Ruddigore* as Zorah. She later made a
great success as the original Nita in Gilbert and
Cellier's *Mountebanks*.

Je ne sais quoi ("A *je-ne-sais-quoi* young man." Pat. 2).
—French colloquial phrase ("I know not what"),
meaning "indescribable."

Jiminy ("Oh, Jiminy." G.D. 2).—A form of "Gemini,"
used formerly as a mild kind of oath. It is said to
be a corruption of Jesu Domine.

J

Jink ("Some at . . . jink." G. 2).—Usually used in the plural. "High jinks" originally meant pranks played at a drinking orgy.

JOHNSTON, EDITH.—Created the part of Salata in *Utopia Ltd.*

Joint Stock Company's Act (U. 1).—This is now to some extent obsolete, being superseded by the Companies (Consolidation) Act of 1908–12. Consequently, some of Gilbert's business allusions are out of date. For instance, it is no longer necessary to have seven persons for the registration of a company.

Jorum ("A jorum of tea." S. 1).—A jorum is a wooden cup, but sometimes the word is used to denote the contents of it.

JOSEPHINE (Pin.).—Captain Corcoran's daughter, whom the First Lord of the Admiralty seeks in marriage, but who is in love with Ralph Rackstraw.

JUDGE, THE LEARNED (T. by J.).—The breach of promise case Angelina *v.* Edwin becoming complicated, he solves the matter by marrying the Plaintiff himself.

Jullien ("The science of Jullien, the eminent musico." Pat. 1).—From the Colonel's Song. Louis Antoine Jullien (1812–1860) was a fantastic and somewhat over-pretentious conductor who came to London in 1838 to escape his creditors, and founded a popular orchestra. He died insane. His "British Army" Quadrilles were still popular at the time of the production of *Patience*.

Jumping Joan (Y. 1).—One of Jack Point's dances. The dance is not known, but there was an old nursery rhyme of that title. Also, there was a dancing figure worked by strings called "Jumping John."

Junket ("Some at junket." G. 2).—A feast. Sometimes used specifically to denote a general feast at the public's expense.

Juvenal ("And the works of Juvenal." P.I. 2).—The famous Roman satirist, of the time of Domitian and Trajan.

K

Kalends ("the Kalends that are Greek," G.D. 2).—
The first day of each month in the Roman Calen-
dar. As there are no Greek Kalends, this is tanta-
mount to saying "Never at all."

KALYBA, THE PRINCESS (U.).—One of the two younger
daughters of King Paramount.

KATE (i) (Pir.).—One of Major-General Stanley's
daughters. (ii) (Y.).—Dame Carruthers' niece, who
takes the soprano part in the Quartet, "Strange
Adventure."

KATISHA (M.).—An elderly lady of the Mikado's
Court, in love with Nanki-Poo. Ko-Ko succeeds in
marrying her to save himself from execution.

KAVANAGH, NELLIE.—Appeared in the original
production of *Ruddigore* as Ruth; and of *The
Gondoliers* as Fiametta.

K.C.B.—Knight Grand Commander of the Order of
the Bath. The Most Honourable Order of the Bath
dates from 1399, and is the second oldest British
Order, that of the Most Noble Order of the Garter
dating from 1349. The ribbon is crimson. The
K.C.B. is the second highest grade, the first being
the Knight Grand Cross (G.C.B.). It is conferred
on military officers and eminent civilians, including
officers of the senior (Naval) Service. There are
three K.C.B.'s in the operas: Sir Marmaduke
Pointdextre (S.); Sir Joseph Porter (Pin.); and
Sir Edward Corcoran (U.).

Keep ("I was born in the old Keep." Y. 1).—The main building of the Tower of London, commonly known as the White Tower.

KELLEHER, MR.—Appeared in the original production of *Trial by Jury* as the Usher.

KENNINGHAM, CHARLES.—Created the parts of Captain Fitzbattleaxe in *Utopia Ltd.* and of Ernest Dummkopf in *The Grand Duke*. He succeeded Courtice Pounds in the first series of revivals.

Kensington Gore.—The title first suggested for *Ruddigore* was "Kensington Gore," or "Robin and Richard were two pretty men."

Kettle of fish ("Here's a pretty kettle of fish." I. 2).—This is a verbatim quotation from Fielding's *Joseph Andrews*.

KING GAMA (P.I.).—Princess Ida's father. See "Hungary."

King George ("In good King George's glorious days." I. 2).—From Mountararat's Song. King George III.

KING HILDEBRAND (P.I.).—Prince Hilarion's father.

KING PARAMOUNT THE FIRST (U.).—King of Utopia.

Kings.—The Kings in the operas are Gama and Hildebrand (P.I.), Luiz of Barataria (G.), and Paramount (U.). The Pirate King (Pir.) is merely self-styled, while Marco and Giuseppe (G.) are Kings by mistake.

Kirtle ("I'll swallow my kirtle." Y. 2).—In Tudor times a kirtle consisted of bodice and petticoat combined.

Knightsbridge (M. 2).—The place to which, in the original production, Ko-Ko says that Nanki-Poo has gone. The reason of this was that in 1885 there was an exhibition at Knightsbridge called the Japanese Village. This is one of the few lines in the operas which Gilbert allowed to be altered, for topical allusions. Such variations have been North Manchester (where Mr. Winston Churchill was seeking election), Locarno, Geneva, White City, Wembley, etc. Knightsbridge is also mentioned in U. 1. ("Knightsbridge nursemaids"), on account of the propinquity of the Guards' Barracks.

Kodaks ("To diagnose our modest pose, the Kodaks do their best." U. 1).—This reference to the snapshot cameras of a famous company is not the only gratuitous advertisement extended by Gilbert, e.g. "Morris wall papers" (G.D. 1).

Ko-Ko (M.).—The Lord High Executioner of Titipu, engaged to his ward Yum-Yum, but subsequently marrying Katisha.

Krakenfeldt, Baroness Von (G.D.).—Betrothed to the Grand Duke Rudolph. Her Christian name is Caroline.

L

Lady Circe's Piggy-wigs (P.I. 2).—Circe was the siren who, on the Island of Aeaea, changed the companions of Odysseus into swine. (*Gr. Myth.*)

Lady Novelist ("That singular anomaly, the lady novelist." M. 1).—As in the case of "Knightsbridge" above, this line has often been varied. We have had "scorching motorist," "fighting Suffragist," "prohibitionist," psycho-analyst," etc.

LAIDLAW, W. S.—Appeared in the original production of *The Gondoliers* as Giuseppe.

Lambeth Walk, No. 8, Boswell Terrace.—The house, in South London, where Sullivan was born.

LA RUE, LILIAN.—Created the part of Kate in *The Pirates of Penzance* (London). Also appeared in the original production of *Pinafore* as Hebe.

LAWRENCE, NELLIE.—Created the part of Fiametta in *The Gondoliers*. Also appeared in the original production of *The Yeomen of the Guard* as Kate, and of *The Gondoliers* as Gianetta.

Legal Characters.—The legal characters in the operas are: Judge, Counsel, Associate, Usher and Barrister (T. by J.); Notary (S.); Sergeant and Constables (Pir.); Mr. Bunthorne's Solicitor (Pat.); Lord Chancellor and his train-bearer (I.); Pooh-Bah (in various capacities) and Ko-Ko (M.); Wilfred Shadbolt (Y.); Don Alhambra (Grand Inquisitor) (G.); Scaphio and Phantis, Tarara, and Sir Bailey Barre (U.); and Dr. Tannhäuser (G.D.).

L

LE HAY, JOHN.—Created the part of Phantis in *Utopia Ltd.* He also appeared as James (*q.v.*) in the Paignton production of *The Pirates of Penzance* sixteen years previously.

LEILA (I.).—One of Strephon's Fairy Aunts. She subsequently allies herself to Lord Tolloller.

LEITCH, GEORGE.—Appeared in the original production of *Trial by Jury* as the Learned Judge.

LELY, DURWARD.—Created the parts of the Duke of Dunstable in *Patience*; Tolloller in *Iolanthe*; Cyril in *Princess Ida*; Nanki-Poo in *The Mikado*; and Richard Dauntless in *Ruddigore*. Also appeared in the original (London) production of *The Pirates of Penzance* as Frederic. Succeeded (Sir) George Power as principal tenor, and was succeeded by Courtice Pounds.

LE MAISTRE, H.—Appeared in the original production of *The Gondoliers* as Luiz.

Leman.—("The lily-white laughing leman." G.D. 2). An expression used by Chaucer, Shakespeare, and Spenser, meaning a lover of either sex, generally in a bad sense.

LEON, W. H.—Appeared in the original production of *Utopia Ltd.* as Scaphio.

LEWIS, ERIC.—Appeared in the original production of *The Mikado* as Ko-Ko.

LEWIS, RUDOLPH.—Created the parts of Old Adam in *Ruddigore* and of the Fourth Citizen in *The Yeomen of the Guard*.

Limited Liability ("The limited liability principle." U. 2).—The Companies Act of 1862 restricted liability to the amount of the declared capital.

LINDSAY, MISS.—Created the part of Ruth in *Ruddigore*. Also appeared in the same original production as Zorah.

Little Ease ("Is the Little Ease sufficiently uncomfortable?" Y. 1).—A form of torture in the Tower of London, consisting of a cell so small that the prisoner could neither lie down nor stand up.

Lord Chancellor (I.).—The husband of Iolanthe, who, believing himself to be a widower, seeks an alliance with his ward in Chancery, Phyllis.

Lord Chancellor's Train-bearer (I.).—This character was not mentioned in the original cast. He appears at the Lord Chancellor's first entry and steps and jumps simultaneously with him during his first song.

Lordship ("Though his lordship's station's mighty"; "For the union of his (my) lordship." Pin. 2).— The title of "lordship" is not granted to a British First Lord of the Admiralty, unless, of course, he happens to be a Peer of the Realm.

Lothario ("An out-and-out Lothario." R. 1).—From the character of that name in Nicholas Rowe's tragedy, *The Fair Penitent*. Generically, anyone noted for his gallantries.

LOUIS, MINNA.—Appeared in the original production of *Patience* both as Patience and Lady Ella; and of *Iolanthe* both as Phyllis and Celia.

L

Louis Quatorze Wig (G.D. 1).—The long curly wig
of natural colour made fashionable by Louis XIV
of France.

LOVEDAY, ELINOR.—Appeared in the original
production of *Pinafore* as Josephine.

"Love that makes the world go round." (I. 2).—It
may be a surprise to learn that this saying, which
is now recognized as one of the proverbs of the day,
is actually Gilbert's own. It is his original paraphrase of the old adage: " 'Tis drink, and only
drink, that makes the world go round," from
Hurdis's *Village Curate* (1797).

Lucius Junius Brutus ("My father, the Lucius Junius
Brutus of his race." M. 1).—First Consul of Rome
who, putting patriotism before paternity, executed
his own sons for conspiring to restore the Tarquins.

LUDWIG (G.D.).—Chief comedian in Ernest Dummkopf's Company, who, for a day, becomes Grand
Duke.

LUGG, WILLIAM.—Created the part of Scynthius
in *Princess Ida*.

LUIZ (G.).—The Duke of Plaza-Toro's "suite," in
love with Casilda, who is, in reality, the King of
Barataria.

LUTZ, MEYER.—The famous conductor of the old
Gaiety Theatre, who directed the production of
Thespis.

LYSTER, E.—Appeared in the first (London) production of *The Pirates of Penzance* as Samuel; and
of *Patience* as Major Murgatroyd.

LYTTON, (SIR) HENRY.—Appeared in the original production of *Ruddigore* as Robin. Although he never created any of the original parts, he has played more than any other Savoyard, and was a member of the touring company as long ago as the production of *Princess Ida* in 1884. He has played every one of the "Grossmith" roles and the Duke of Plaza-Toro in *The Gondoliers*. Moreover, he has played many of the other parts in addition, including the Judge (T. by J.), Dick Deadeye (Pin.), the Pirate King (Pir.), Strephon (I.), and Wilfred Shadbolt (Y.) in the first revival of 1897. He also created several non-Gilbert and Sullivan parts at the Savoy Theatre, including Prince Paul in *The Grand Duchess*, the Earl of Essex in *Merrie England*, and Jelf in *A Princess of Kensington*. He celebrated the fiftieth anniversary of his connection with the Savoy operas on February 5, 1934. Lady Lytton (Louie Henri) appeared as Tessa in a revival of *The Gondoliers* at the Savoy. (See Notes on *Ruddigore*.)

M

MABEL (Pir.).—Major-General Stanley's daughter who allies herself to the Pirate Apprentice, Frederic.

Macaulay ("Wit of Macaulay who wrote of Queen Anne." Pat. 1).—From the Colonel's Song. Lord Macaulay is not reckoned as a wit, but a serious historian and essayist. Moreover, he wrote little about the reign of Queen Anne.

McINTOSH, NANCY.—Created the part of Princess Zara in *Utopia Ltd*. She became Sir William and Lady Gilbert's adopted daughter.

Madrigal.—Ralph's opening song in Act I (Pin.) is called a Madrigal, but it is not happily named, the madrigalian form being for several parts. The Madrigals in (R.) and (M.) are fine examples, though Sullivan, with characteristic modesty, called the latter merely "a poor little part-song."

Madame Louise ("We're Madame Louise young girls." Pat. 2).—A famous milliner in Regent Street, reputed to have been the mother of a well-known theatrical family. There was also a dress-making establishment of that name in New Bond Street.

Madame Tussaud.—(i) Mentioned in the Colonel's Song (Pat. 1). (ii) "At Madame Tussaud's wax-work" (M. 2). This famous exhibition was established shortly after the French Revolution, Madame Tussaud, as a young girl skilled in making casts, being actually compelled to make such models of the heads of the guillotine victims. She came to England early in the last century and, after exhibiting in the provinces, settled in London, and for many years her Exhibition was in Upper Baker Street. It was removed to its present site in Marylebone Road in 1884, was burnt out in 1925, and rebuilt, and remains to this day one of the sights of London particularly attractive to provincial visitors.

MAD MARGARET (R.).—A wild village maiden in love with Sir Despard Murgatroyd, who marries her after the Witch's Curse is removed from him. See "Titled Characters."

Main-truck ("Whether he hoists his flag at the main-truck." Pin. 1).—A small wooden cup at the summit of a mast-head, with holes for receiving halyards. (*Naut.*)

Mamelon ("When I know what is meant by 'mamelon.'" Pir. 1).—A hillock or mound suitable for ambush, sniping, etc. (*Mil.*)

MANDEVILLE, ALICE.—Appeared in the original production of *Pinafore* as Josephine.

Manfred ("Little of Manfred but not very much of him." Pat. 1).—From the Colonel's Song. This may refer to (i) the King of Naples and Sicily who fell in the Battle of Benevento, A.D. 1266, or (ii) the hero in Byron's play of that name, who repents of his life as a necromancer.

MANNERS, CHARLES.—Created the part of Private Willis in *Iolanthe*. He married the operatic soprano, Fanny Moody, and with her organized the Moody-Manners Opera Company.

M

Manzanilla (G. 2).—From the Cachucha chorus. A light sherry, one of the favourite wines in Spain. From Manzanilla, camomile.

Marathon ("I can quote the fights historical from Marathon to Waterloo." Pir. 1).—Battle between the Greeks and the Persians. The Marathon race, a term now used in connection with long-distance running, was the effort made by a courier to convey the news of the victory of the Greeks to Athens. He ran the whole distance, twenty-two miles, gave his message, and then dropped dead.

Maravedi ("Is not worth a maravedi." I. 2).—A Spanish copper coin worth about a thirteenth of a penny. It was first minted in 1848.

March of the Mikado's Troops (M. 2).—This is an adaptation, words and music, of the War Song of the Japanese Imperial Army of 1868, used during the Sino-Japanese War. Sullivan's music is approximately the same; Gilbert's words absolutely so, except for the dividing up of some of the syllables.

MARCHMONT, MR.—Appeared in the original production of *The Mikado* as Pish-Tush.

MARCO (G.).—One of the reputed sons of Baptisto Palmieri, who reigns temporarily with his brother Giuseppe as King of Barataria, married to Gianetta.

MARIUS, MONSIEUR.—Appeared as the Defendant in the original production of *Trial by Jury*. Became a popular light opera tenor, playing chiefly with his wife, Florence St. John.

Mark (Y. 1).—The English mark, a coin of pure silver, was worth two-thirds of a pound, 13s. 4d.

"Marriage with deceased wife's sister" (I. 1).—A famous Bill, for many years a bone of contention in Parliament, to make valid the marriage of a widower and his sister-in-law. It became a legalized Act in 1907.

"Marry, come up" (P.I. 2).—Originally "Mary, go up," an oath referring to the Virgin. It is to be found in Cowley's poem, "The Cutler of Coleman Street," 1663.

MARTHA (G.D.).—One of Dummkopf's theatrical company.

Matadoro ("Count Matadoro." G. 1).—One of the titles of the Duke of Plaza-Toro. All his titles are redolent of a Spanish bull-fight. The Matador is the official who waves a red handkerchief before the bull, to infuriate it.

Mauser rifle (Pir. 1).—This term is generally substituted for that of "chassepôt" in the Major-General's patter song.

Maxim gun ("Their Empire-shaking blows have dealt with Maxim gun. . . ." U. 1).—A quick-firing machine gun invented by Hiram Maxim, and adopted by the British Army four years before the production of *Utopia Ltd.*

MAY, ALICE.—Created the part of Aline in *The Sorcerer* and of Josephine in *Pinafore*.

MAYBUD, ROSE (R.).—A village maiden, niece of Dame Hannah. Although in love with Robin Oakapple, she is a self-seeking coquette, and, during the opera, actually proposes to Sir Despard and to Richard Dauntless.

MAYNARD, ELSIE (Y.).—A strolling player beloved by her partner, Jack Point. Blindfolded, she marries Colonel Fairfax in the Coldharbour Tower.

MELENE (U.).—A Utopian maiden.

MELISSA (P.I.).—Lady Blanche's daughter, who allies herself to Florian.

"Melt a rich uncle in wax." (S. 1.).—From the mediaeval belief that the melting of a waxen image of a person caused his death.

MENTONE, VISCOUNT (G.D. 2).—One of the Prince of Monte Carlo's pseudo-peers.

Mephisto ("Force of Mephisto pronouncing a ban." Pat. 1).—From the Colonel's Song.

Mephistopheles Minor (U. 1).—The pseudonym adopted by the King, for his article, "Where is the Public Exploder?" written by him under compulsion in *The Palace Peeper*.

Mercury Major (U. 1).—The pseudonym adopted by the King for "Ribald Royalty." See "Mephistopheles Minor."

Merovingian ("An antique . . . of the early Merovingian period." G.D. 2).—The Prince of Monte Carlo's description of the Baroness von Krakenfeldt. The Merovingians were rulers of France between the years 500 and 750. The last, Childeric III, was deposed by Pepin in 751.

MERTON, MR.—Created the part of the Third Yeoman in *The Yeomen of the Guard*.

MERYLL, LEONARD (Y.).—Sergeant Meryll's son, appointed a Warder of the Tower.

MERYLL, PHOEBE (Y.).—Sergeant Meryll's daughter, who helps to effect Fairfax's escape by taking from Wilfred Shadbolt the key of his cell.

MERYLL, SERGEANT (Y.).—Of the Yeomen of the Guard. To save himself, he proposes to Dame Carruthers, who has discovered the plot to save Colonel Fairfax.

METCALF, MR.—Sometimes appearing on the programmes as Medcalf. Created the parts of Second Citizen in *The Yeomen of the Guard* and of Antonio in *The Gondoliers*.

Micawber, Mr. (Pat. 1).—The famous Dickens character in *David Copperfield*. Mentioned in the Colonel's Song.

MIKADO OF JAPAN, THE (M.).—His immortal policy of "letting the punishment fit the crime" is hinted at by King Paramount in *Utopia Ltd*, who says that he is in constant communication with the Mikado as a leading authority on punishments.

MIKADO, THE, or *THE TOWN OF TITIPU*.— The eighth opera. Produced at the Savoy Theatre, March 14, 1885, and ending its original run on January 19, 1887, the number of performances being 672. It was revived in 1888, 1895, 1896, and 1908, the aggregate performances, 1,183 in all, easily constituting a record for any one opera.

NOTES ON "THE MIKADO"

In the Mikado's Song, at the words "With Bach and Beethoven," Sullivan introduces the first twelve notes of Bach's great Fugue in G minor, played by bassoon and clarinet.

Wednesday, March 10, 1886, was a notable day. It was the first time in the history of the modern stage that performances were permitted on Ash Wednesday. The restriction had been removed officially on September 29, 1885.

In face of the "*Mikado* ban" of later years (*q.v.*), it is interesting to note that the original production was witnessed on December 10, 1886, by the Japanese Prince Komatsa, who saw no offence in it.

Mikado Ban.—A short time before the close of Mrs. D'Oyly Carte's tenure of the Savoy Theatre, it was rumoured that the opera had been objected to by certain Japanese naval officers. Consequently it was removed temporarily from the repertoire. At her final performances in August 1909 great enthusiasm was kindled by Mr. François Cellier's conducting of the *Overture* only.

Millais ("Viscount Millais . . . we'll welcome sweetly." U. 2).—Sir John Millais, the famous artist, whose "Bubbles" was used, in reproduction, for Pears' Soap, had already been knighted in 1885.

Military Characters.—The military characters in the operas are: Alexis (Grenadier Guards) (S.); Major-General Stanley (Pir.); Sergeant and Guard of Royal Marines (Pin.); Colonel Calverley, Major Murgatroyd, Lieutenant the Duke of Dunstable, and Squadron (Dragoon Guards) (Pat.); Private Willis (Grenadier Guards) (I.); Arac, Guron, and Scynthius and men (P.I.); Pooh-Bah (Commander-in-Chief, etc.) (M.); Officers representing various regiments in the Peninsular War (R.); Colonel Fairfax, Leonard Meryll, Sergeant Meryll, and ex-Service Warders (Y.); Captain Fitzbattleaxe and Four Troopers (Life Guards) (U.). Frederic (Pir.), although attired in undress Cavalry uniform in Act II, cannot belong to the Army.

Miminy-piminy ("Francesca di Rimini, miminy-piminy." Pat. 2).—A phrase meaning finicky or fastidious. It was used by Mrs. Pilkington and by Hazlitt more than a hundred years ago.

Minerva ("Minerva. . . . O Goddess wise." P.I. 2).— Minerva was the Roman goddess (in Greece, Pallas Athene) of wisdom, sense, reflection, arts, poetry, and sciences.

Mistress Lalage (P.I. 2).—The hostess of "The Pigeons," where Hilarion and his friends used to resort. Mentioned by Cyril when under the influence of wine.

Monarchs.—The Monarchs and their Consorts mentioned in the operas are: Queen Anne (Pat. 1); King Arthur (Pir. 1); Queen Elizabeth (I. 2); George III (I. 2); Henry VIII (implied) (Y. 1); James II (T. by J.); the Empress Josephine (Pat. 1); Louis XIV of France (G.D. 1); Napoleon Buonaparte (I. 2); Victor Emmanuel of Italy (Pat. 1); and Queen Victoria (Pir. 2).

MONTE CARLO, PRINCE OF (G.D.).—Father of the Princess of Monte Carlo, whom he brings to be wedded, according to contract, to the Grand Duke Rudolph.

MONTE CARLO, PRINCESS OF (G.D.).—The Prince of Monte Carlo's daughter, who is betrothed to the Grand Duke Rudolph.

MONTELLI, MR.—Appeared as Bill Bobstay in the original production of *Pinafore*.

Montero (G. 2).—Spanish wine, derived from the same word meaning a mountaineer, and used largely in the Spanish Pyrenees.

MOORE, DECIMA.—Created the part of Casilda in *The Gondoliers*. See Notes on the original production.

Mop and mow ("Away they go with a mop and a mow." R. 2).—Both words mean "a grimace." The expression occurs as long ago as 1581, when Pettie wrote that the ape "makes us laugh with his mops and mows."

Morra (G. 2).—One of the games played by the courtiers of Barataria. It has always been a favourite one in Italy. Two players face each other and alternately raise their hands quickly while each *vis-à-vis* guesses how many fingers are held up by the other. The one who first guesses nine times correctly takes the stakes. It has the advantage, being without accessories, of being able to be played anywhere.

Morris ("From Ovid and Horace to Swinburne and Morris." R. 1).—William Morris, poet and member of the Pre-Raphaelites, was born in 1834 and died in 1896. See "Grosvenor Gallery."

Morris wall papers (G.D. 1).—William Morris revived the tapestry style of wall decoration in 1862, his patterns including Daisies, Trellis-work, Pomegranates, and Acanthi. Incidentally, that was a hundred years after the Grand Duke's time.

MORTON, CHARLES.—The Manager at the Royalty Theatre when the third portion of the original production of *Trial by Jury* was presented. He subsequently became famous as Manager of the Palace Theatre of Varieties.

MOUNTARARAT, EARL OF (I.).—One of the two Peers who become engaged to Phyllis, but who eventually allies himself to Celia. His Christian name is George.

MURGATROYD, MAJOR (Pat.).—Of the 35th Dragoon Guards. He subsequently allies himself to Lady Angela.

MURGATROYD, SIR CONRAD (R.).—Twelfth Baronet of Ruddigore.

MURGATROYD, SIR DESMOND (R.).—Sixteenth Baronet of Ruddigore.

MURGATROYD, SIR DESPARD (R.).—Sir Ruthven Murgatroyd's younger brother, who, believing the latter to be dead, succeeds to the Baronetcy of Ruddigore and its attendant curse. Later becomes virtuous and marries Mad Margaret.

MURGATROYD, SIR GILBERT (R.).—Eighteenth Baronet of Ruddigore.

MURGATROYD, SIR JASPER (R.).—Third Baronet of Ruddigore.

MURGATROYD, SIR LIONEL (R.).—Sixth Baronet of Ruddigore.

M

MURGATROYD, SIR MERVYN (R.).—Twentieth Baronet of Ruddigore.

MURGATROYD, SIR RODERIC (R.).—Twenty-first Baronet of Ruddigore. Sir Ruthven's Uncle, betrothed in his lifetime to Dame Hannah.

MURGATROYD, SIR RUTHVEN (R.).—Twenty-second Baronet of Ruddigore. Until unmasked by his brother Despard, he evades his title and its responsibilities by masquerading under the name of Robin Oakapple (*q.v.*).

Musical instruments.—The following instruments are used or are mentioned in the operas: banjo (U. 2); bells (S. 1); bones (U. 2); castanets (G. 2); citherae (G.D. 1); clarion (G. 2); cornet-à-piston (G. 1); cymbals (Pat. 2); drum (P.I.; R. 1; G. 1); fiddle (R. 1; G. 1); flageolet (S. 2); flute (Y. 1; U. 1; G.D. 1); guitar (T. by J.); harp (Pat. 1); hurdy-gurdy (P.I. 3); Japanese guitar (E. 1); lute (Pat, 1; U. 1); lyre (G. 1; U. 1); mandolin (Pin. 2; G. 1); organ (Pin. 2); Pan pipe (Pat. 2); shepherd's pipe (I. 1); tabor (I. 1); tambourine (U. 1); triangle (U. 2); trombone (R. 1); trumpet (Pir. 2; I. 1; R. 1); violoncello (or double bass) (Pat. 2).

Musicians.—The following musicians are mentioned in the operas: Bach (M. 2); Beethoven (M. 2); Jullien (Pat. 1); Offenbach (implied) (G.D. 1); Spohr (M. 2); Sullivan (implied) (Pir. 1); Wagner (P.I. 3).

Mystical Germans ("Mystical Germans who preach from ten to four." M. 2).—The practice of preaching long-winded sermons was prevalent with certain German divines at the time of *The Mikado*.

N

Nanki-Poo (M.).—The Mikado's Son, disguised as a wandering minstrel, in love with Yum-Yum.

Nannikin (R. 2).—Sir Roderic Murgatroyd's pet name for Dame Hannah.

Narcissus ("I am a very Narcissus." Pat. 2).—The beautiful youth who died of admiration of his own features reflected in a pool. (*Gr. Myth.*)

Nativity (S. 1).—The astrological estimate of birth, akin to a horoscope.

Naval Characters.—The following are the naval characters in the operas: Sir Joseph Porter (First Lord of the Admiralty), Captain Corcoran, Bill Bobstay, Bob Becket, Ralph Rackstraw, Tommy Tucker (Midshipman), Dick Deadeye, and the remainder of the ship's crew (Pin.); Pooh-Bah (First Lord of the Admiralty) (M.); Richard Dauntless (R.); and Sir Edward Corcoran (U.). The Sergeant and men of the Royal Marines (Pin.) are half naval, while the Pirate King, Samuel, Frederic, and the pirate crew are at least seafaring men.

Necromancy ("We practise Necromancy." S. 1).— Derived from νεκρός, a dead body (*Gr.*). The black art, that is, divination by communication with the dead.

Nekaya, The Princess (U.).—One of Princess Zara's young sisters.

Nelson ("The pluck of Lord Nelson on board of the *Victory*." Pat. 1).—From the Colonel's Song.

Neophytes ("Women of Adamant, fair Neophytes." P.I. 2).—From the Greek, meaning "newly-planted." New converts, novices, or probationers.

Nineteen-forty ("That birthday will not be reached till 1940." Pir. 2).—The date of Frederic's birth, and, consequently, the date on which the opera is supposed to take place, are harder to determine than might be supposed. Gilbert obviously forgot that the year 1900 was not a Leap Year. Were it so, the opera would take place in 1877. That is the date which one may reasonably suppose to be the one intended, 1876 being the Leap Year nearest to that in which the opera was written. But, as 1900 has to be omitted, a little arithmetical calculation will show that (i) the time of the opera was 1873; (ii) Frederic was twenty-one years of age in that year; (iii) he was born in 1852; (iv) consequently he was over six in 1877; and (v) if 1877 had really been the right year, he would not reach his twenty-first birthday until 1944.

Nisi Prius ("That Nisi Prius nuisance." M. 1) (*Lat.*). —Pronounced with all the "i"s long. It means "unless before," and constitutes a legal fiction. Certain provincial law suits are supposed to be heard in London, with a jury selected from the town where the cases arise. In order to save trouble and expense, these cases are tried at the local Assizes by the High Court Judge on circuit. They are, however. entered for hearing at the Royal

Courts of Justice, "unless" they have been heard "before." As the date of the London trial is invariably arranged after the date of the Assize sessions, they are tried by the Assize Judge, who is called, therefore, a Nisi Prius Judge.

NOEL, MR.—Appeared as Ralph Rackstraw in the original production of *Pinafore*.

No-fee system.—This was adopted for the first time in stage history by D'Oyly Carte, at the opening of the Savoy Theatre, followed by the Management of the Gaiety Theatre. These were the only two theatres where the system was adopted in its entirety, namely:—no charges for programmes, no fees for cloak-room attendance, and no gratuities.

"None but the brave deserve the fair" (I. 2).—A direct quotation from Dryden's *Alexander's Feast*.

Nordenfelt ("With Maxim gun and Nordenfelt." U. 1). Machine gun designed especially for naval use.

Nosology ("Mystic nosology." S. 1).—The science of diseases.

NOTARY (S.).—A sixty-six-year-old lawyer who draws up the marriage settlement between Alexis and Aline, with whom Constance, after taking the potion, falls in love. There is also a Notary in *The Grand Duke*. See "Tannhäuser, Dr."

"Nothing in particular" ("Did nothing in particular and did it very well." I. 2).—Possibly suggested by Cowper's "Doing nothing with a great deal of skill," from *Table Talk*.

N

"Nothing venture, nothing win" (I. 2).—The original saying is "Naught venture, naught have" from Thomas Tusser's *Five Points of Good Husbands*. Similar phrases are to be found in Latin, French, Italian, and Spanish.

OAKAPPLE, ROBIN (R.).—The name under which Sir Ruthven Murgatroyd, the twenty-second baronet of Ruddigore, conceals his identity, in order to escape the family curse.

Oboloi ("I'll pay 'em, if they'll back me, all in *oboloi*. . . ." G.D. 2).—Athenian coins worth about the sixth of a *drachma*. See *"Drachmae."*

Odalesque ("Grace of an Odalesque on a divan." Pat. 1).—From the Colonel's Song. A female slave or member of a Turkish harem.

Ods bobs, Ods bodikins (Y. 2).—"Od" is a corruption of "God," and is therefore a form of oath, the phrases originally meaning respectively "God's curls" and "God's dear body."

Oldest Characters.—The oldest characters of which the age is definitely known are the Notary (S.) and Scaphio (U.), both of whom are sixty-six. The oldest woman to disclose her age is Ruth (Pir.), who is forty-seven. But several other ladies must be older than that. Lady Sangazure (S.) was loved by Sir Marmaduke forty years ago, while, of immortals, Iolanthe is said to be "a couple of centuries or so."

OLGA (G.D.).—One of the members of Ernest Dummkopf's theatrical company.

"One is a tenor, two are baritones" (P.I. 2).—This is incorrect. Hilarion and Cyril are both tenors. As the libretto was written before the music, it would seem that the slip was Sullivan's in writing Cyril's numbers for a tenor voice.

One Tree Hill ("I often roll down One Tree Hill." S. 2).—A hill in Greenwich Park which was often "rolled down" in the days of Greenwich Fair. There is also a rise of that name near Honor Oak Park, not far from Greenwich in the S.E. district of London.

Opera Comique.—This theatre was the birthplace of *The Sorcerer*, *Pinafore*, *Pirates of Penzance* (London), and *Patience*. It was opened in 1870, and pulled down in 1901.

Opoponax (G.D. 2).—Used in the opera merely as a convenient word for chorus-singing. It is the juice of the herb panex, so-called from the Greek ὅπος, juice, and πάναξ, a plant. Strictly speaking, therefore, the real word is spelt with the third "o" as "a."

Ordeal ("Of an ordeal by battle." P.I. 3).—Here Gilbert reverts to the original pronunciation, of three syllables—"or-de-al."

Otto ("Breathing concentrated Otto." T. by J.).— The scent known correctly as "Attar of Roses," distilled from rose petals. It is obtained chiefly from the Balkan States.

Ovid ("From Ovid and Horace." R. 1).—It is important to remember that the "O" is short, and that the name is pronounced "Ovvid." See "Ovidius Naso."

Ovidius Naso (I. 2).—Ovidius Naso (Ovid) was the famous Latin amatory poet, 43 B.C.–A.D. 17. He was nicknamed Naso owing to his big nose. See "Amorous Dove."

Ovid's Metamorphoses (P.I. 2).—The most famous of Ovid's works. They describe mythical events from the beginning of the world to the age of Caesar.

OWEN, EMMIE.—Created the parts of Nekaya in *Utopia Ltd.* and of the Princess of Monte Carlo in *The Grand Duke.* She also played many of the leads in revivals. Her name first appeared on the programmes as Amy Owens.

P

Paddington Pollaky ("Keen penetration of Paddington
Pollaky." Pat. 1).—From the Colonel's Song. A
celebrated detective of Victorian times, attached
to the Paddington Police Office. He may be said
to have represented the transitional stage from the
Bow-Street Runners to the C.I.D.

Paget ("Coolness of Paget about to trepan." Pat. 1).
—From the Colonel's Song. Sir James Paget, the
eminent surgeon, was at the height of his fame when
Patience was produced. He was created a Baronet in
1871, was President of the Royal College of Surgeons in 1875, and died in 1899.

Palace Peeper, The (U. 1).—A scurrilous journal
edited, under the compulsion of Scaphio and
Phantis, by the King himself.

PALLISER, ESTHER.—This famous vocalist appeared in the original production of *The Gondoliers*
as Gianetta.

PALMAY, ILKA VON.—Created the part of Julia
Jellicoe in *The Grand Duke*. She was a Hungarian
noblewoman.

Pandean ("Gaily pipe Pandean pleasure." Pat. 1).—
Pertaining to the god Pan. Pronounced "Pan-
dee-an."

Paragon ("Paragon of common sense." P.I. 2).—
Originally meaning "an equal," it has become a
term for a "pattern" or "model." Compare
Shakespeare: "Man, the paragon of animals."

Parliamentary Trains ("To ride on the buffer of Parliamentary trains." M. 2).—An ordinary passenger train on one of the accredited lines, conforming to the statutory rate of fare, established by Parliament, of one penny a mile.

PARRY, CHARLES.—Appeared as the Counsel for the Plaintiff in the original production of *Trial by Jury*.

PARTLET, MRS. (S.).—A pew opener, with whom Sir Marmaduke Pointdextre, after taking the love potion, falls in love. Her Christian name is Zorah.

PASSMORE, WALTER.—Created the parts of Tarara in *Utopia Ltd.* and of the Grand Duke Rudolph in *The Grand Duke*. He subsequently was recognized as the first great successor of Grossmith, and played all his characters. He also created many original parts in other works at the Savoy, chief of which was Walter Wilkins in *Merrie England*.

PATIENCE (Pat.).—A milkmaid. Betrothed to Reginald Bunthorne from a sense of duty, she eventually returns to her early playmate, Archibald Grosvenor.

PATIENCE, or *BUNTHORNE'S BRIDE*.—Fifth opera. Produced at the Opera Comique on April 23, 1881, and removed to the Savoy Theatre on its opening night, October 10, 1881, where it ran till November 22, 1882, with a total of 578 performances. Revived in 1900 and 1907, the aggregate number of performances being 779.

NOTES ON "PATIENCE"

The new-comers at the first production were Leonora Braham, from the German Reed's Entertainment at St. George's Hall, and Mabel Fortescue, the sister of Helen Ferrers, who made her stage début in this opera.

_____

The opera, a satire on the Oscar Wilde aesthetic cult, was founded on a Bab Ballad concerning the Rev. Clayton Hooper, of Spoffington-extra-Soper, and the Rev. Hopley Porter, of Assesmilk-cum-Water. Aesthetism had previously been satirized by George du Maurier's Mr. Maudle in *Punch*, and by (Sir) F. C. Burnand in his comedy-farce, *The Colonel*, which had been produced shortly before this opera. Lest it should be thought that there was any plagiarism of *The Colonel* in *Patience*, Mr. D'Oyly Carte announced that the libretto of the latter had been completed in the previous November.

_____

As Reginald Bunthorne, Grossmith was made up as a caricature of J. M. Whistler, the pre-Raphaelite artist.

_____

For two coincidences in connection with the Colonel's Song, see "Wolseley" and "Anthony Trollope."

_____

Rutland Barrington, who appeared on the opening night of the Savoy Theatre in 1881, also appeared on the closing night in 1909, the only member of the company to do so.

_____

The last thirteen notes of the melody of the Sextet, "I hear the soft note," in Act I are identical with those of Henry Smart's tune to "Hark, hark, my Soul." Smart died in 1879, so his melody came first.

——————

It is interesting to note that Mrs. D'Oyly Carte, who assisted in this satire, arranged, before her marriage, Oscar Wilde's lecture tours.

PAUL, MRS. HOWARD.—Created the part of Lady Sangazure in *The Sorcerer*. She died on June 6, 1878, and her widower married Letty Lind, the Gaiety Theatre dancer. She was the only lady artist in the Gilbert and Sullivan operas to play under her married name.

"Paw of cat the chestnut snatches" (Pin. 2).—The original monkey who made the cat pull out the chestnuts for him is supposed to have belonged to Pope Julius II (1503–1513). The fable was first in print in Allman's *Guzman d'Alf* (1603).

Paynim ("As an old Crusader struck his Paynim foe." P.I. 3).—Paynim or painim is derived from the word "paganism," and means infidel.

Pecker ("Be firm, my pecker." T. by J.).—Slang for "courage," equivalent to the modern phrase, "Keep a stiff upper lip." It is to be found in Cuthbert Bede's *Verdant Green*.

Peckham ("Peckham an Arcadian vale." T. by J.).— From the Counsel's Song. Even in 1875 Peckham, in South-East London, was a densely populated district.

Peculiarities parabolus (Pir. 1).—From the Major-General's Song. A parabolus is a curve, any point of which is equally distant from a fixed point, the focus, and from a fixed straight line, the directrix. (*Geom.*)

PEEP-BO (M.).—One of the three school-girl wards of Ko-Ko. She eventually allies herself to Pish-Tush.

PEMBERTON, LOUISE.—Appeared in the original production of *The Gondoliers* as Gianetta.

PENLEY, W. S.—The famous originator of the part of *Charley's Aunt*, and the successor to (Sir) Herbert Beerbohm Tree as the Rev. Robert Spalding in *The Private Secretary*, appeared in the original production of *Trial by Jury* in the parts of the Judge, the Foreman, and the Usher. He never played in Gilbert and Sullivan opera at the Savoy Theatre, but he played there in 1892 as Punka in *The Nautch Girl*.

PEPPER, MR.—Created the part of the Usher in *Trial by Jury*.

Peripatetics ("The peripatetics of long-haired Aesthetics." Pat. 1).—From the Colonel's Song, "When I first put this uniform on." The meaning is "Those who walk about," referring specifically to the disciples of Aristotle, who were taught by him whilst walking about the Lyceum at Athens. The word, as an adjective, appears also in the same opera, in Grosvenor's Song, "The Magnet and the Churn."

Perola.—The title originally chosen for the opera *Iolanthe* (*q.v.*).

Perpend ("hold thy peace and perpend." Y. 2).—An

obsolete word, used by Shakespeare, meaning "pay attention."

PERRY, BEATRICE.—Created the part of Martha in *The Grand Duke*.

PERRY, FLORENCE.—Created the parts of Kalyba in *Utopia Ltd.* and Lisa in *The Grand Duke*. She succeeded Jessie Bond as the principal soubrette and played in many revivals.

PETRELLI, EMILIE.—Appeared in the original (London) production of *The Pirates of Penzance* as Mabel.

Pfennig-Halbpfennig (G.D.).—German equivalent for "Penny-halfpenny." The name of the Duchy over which the Grand Duke Rudolph reigned. Dummkopf raises it a grade, for in his theatrical song he calls it a "tuppenny" State.

PHANTIS (U.).—One of the two Judges of the Utopian Supreme Court who hold the King under their thumbs. His age is fifty-five.

Philomel ("Soft the song of Philomel." U. 2).—The nightingale. So called from Philomela, daughter of King Pandion. (*Gr. Myth.*)

PHIPPS, C. J.—The famous theatre architect who designed the Savoy Theatre.

PHYLLA (U.).—A Utopian maiden. She sings the first solo in the opera.

PHYLLIS (I.).—An Arcadian shepherdess, ward in chancery, and in love with Strephon.

Phyllis ("Come, Chloe and Phyllis." R. 1).—Typical

name for a pastoral sweetheart. It first occurs in Virgil's Third Eclogue.

PHYLLIS, N.—Created the part of Giulia in *The Gondoliers*. Also appeared as Gianetta and Vittoria.

Piazzetta (G. 1).—The Scene in Venice for Act I. Italian word meaning a small place or square. The Piazzetta in Venice is on the St. Mark's Canal, with the Doge's Palace and the Royal Palace adjoining.

Picadoro, Baron (G. 1).—One of the Duke of Plaza-Toro's titles. A picador is armed with a lance in a bull fight, and pierces the bull without killing him, the final despatch being allotted to the Toreador.

Pickford ("He's a Parliamentary Pickford." I. 2).— A well-known firm of London parcel carriers. Hence the reference to Strephon's influence in Parliament, where he "carries everything."

Pictures of Ancestors (R.).—The original pictures of the Ruddigore baronets, from which the Ghosts emerged, were painted by Mr. Balard. Each picture was the exact counterpart of the player of the part.

"Pigeons, The" (P.I.).—The hostelry which Cyril says that Prince Hilarion frequented.

Pimpernel (Y. 1).—One of Jack Point's repertoire of dances. It is purely an imaginary one.

PINAFORE, H.M.S., or *THE LASS THAT LOVED A SAILOR.*—Third opera. Produced at the Opera Comique on May 25, 1878. t ran until Friday,

February 20, 1880, with a total of 563 performances. It was revived in 1887, 1899, and 1908,
the aggregate performances being 918.

NOTES ON "PINAFORE"

The new-comers were Emma Howson, a brilliant
operatic soprano, who was the first of the many
Josephines, and Jessie Bond, who was the leading
soubrette of the company for over twelve years.

The official programme of the first production
gives Alice May as the player of Josephine. This
was not so. Miss May and Mr. G. B. Allen (q.v.)
had left the company to assist in the production
of Lecocq's *Little Duke* at the Philharmonic Theatre.

Grossmith never missed a performance during
the whole of the original run.

In some of the provincial performances Gilbert,
anticipating the Suffragists, made some of the
sisters, cousins, and aunts fierce-looking females
who brandished umbrellas.

The present parts of the Boatswain's Mate and
the Carpenter's Mate were originally the Boatswain
and the Boatswain's Mate.

In August 1879 commenced the series of regret-
table wrangles which began with the *Pinafore*
riot (q.v.). The opposing parties were the Comedy
Opera Company and Mr. D'Oyly Carte, who was
supported by the author and composer. Briefly,

the dispute was which party had the right to continue the performances of *Pinafore*. The Company's lease of the theatre had ended, but D'Oyly Carte had secured a lease on his own account. He, therefore, claimed the right to carry on the production, while the Company claimed a similar right to continue the opera at another theatre. The immediate result was that there were presentations of *Pinafore* at two different theatres. After much litigation, D'Oyly Carte won the day, and the Gilbert and Sullivan works remained in his hands. The performances under his management are the only ones considered here.

The "Ruler of the Queen's Navee" was a good-humoured dig at the Right Hon. W. H. Smith (on whose widow was conferred the title of Viscountess Hambleden), who was First Lord at the time. He was, however, never a lawyer's clerk, but the head of the famous book and newspaper agency.

Pinafore Riot.—This occurred on July 31, 1879. For the causes which led to it, see Notes on *Pinafore* above. The Comedy Opera Company, having started an opposition production at the Olympic Theatre, made an attempt to stop the performance at the Opera Comique. Blows were exchanged, and Mr. Richard Barker, the acting manager, was thrown down the stairs, an assault for which he afterwards was awarded damages. Grossmith and Barrington, pluckily carrying on, succeeded in allaying the alarm in the auditorium, but the performance was given amidst great excitement on both sides of the house.

Pɪʀᴀᴛᴇ Kɪɴɢ, Tʜᴇ (Pir.).—The leader of the Pirates of Penzance to whom Frederic is bound apprentice. After he and his band overcome the Police, they surrender in Queen Victoria's name, and the Pirate King obtains Major-General Stanley's consent to his wedding Edith Stanley.

PIRATES OF PENZANCE, THE, or *THE SLAVE OF DUTY.*—Fourth opera. The original London production at the Opera Comique ran from April 3, 1880, till April 2, 1881, with a total of 366 performances. It was revived in 1888, 1900, and 1908, the total aggregate number of performances being 616.

NOTES ON "THE PIRATES OF PENZANCE"

The first production, for copyright purposes, was at Paignton, on December 30, 1879, followed, on the next night, with a production at the Fifth Avenue Theatre, New York. It had, therefore, the unique experience of a Gilbert and Sullivan work being heard in America before appearing in London.

The new-comers in the London production were Marion Hood, later a Gaiety Theatre favourite; George Temple, Richard Temple's brother; and Julia Gwynne (Mrs. George Edwardes).

Helen Everard was billed to create the part of Ruth, but, owing to her sudden illness, her place was taken by Emily Cross. She played the part, however, from June 19th to July 1st.

Major-General Stanley's Song, "Softly sighing to the river," was intended as a piece of purposeful humour. It was thought that some fun might be extracted from Grossmith, who had a poor voice, trying to sing a straight ballad.

———

Owing to sad circumstances, a wonderful record was terminated on April 27, 1880: Grossmith's father died, and thus the creator of Major-General Stanley was absent from the cast until May 2nd. This was the first time that he was out of the bill since his début in 1877, an unbroken period of two and a half years.

———

Rosina Brandram played Kate at the Opera Comique for a short time after her return from the American production.

———

The incident of the defenceless Frederic dooming the armed Pirate King and Ruth to extermination is akin to a situation in Balfe's *Siege of Rochelle*.

———

The opera afforded another instance of unconscious plagiarism. In later times the melody of the music-hall song, "We all go the same way home," sung by Charles Whittle, bears a striking resemblance to that of the Pirates' Chorus.

———

The following lines were originally in the Finale to Act II:

PIRATES
    "To Queen Victoria's name we bow,
        As free-born Britons should.
    We can resist no longer now,
        And would not if we could.
    Hail, House of Peers, all hail, all hail,
    Where wisdom goes in strict entail."

PISH-TUSH (M.).—A noble lord, who allies himself to Peep-Bo. In the Madrigal in Act II his part of the bass in the quartet is sometimes taken by another singer, introduced into the cast as Go-To.

PITTI-SING (M.).—One of Ko-Ko's three schoolgirl wards. One of the accomplices in the deception practised on the Mikado, she is pardoned and allies herself to Pooh-Bah.

PLAINTIFF (T. by J.).—She brings an action for breach of promise against Edwin, but eventually accepts the Judge. See "Edwin and Angelina."

PLAZA-TORO, DUCHESS OF (G.).—Mother of Casilda, the Queen of Barataria, who rules her husband with an iron hand.

PLAZA-TORO, DUKE OF (G.).—A Grandee of Spain and father of Casilda. "Plaza-Toro" means "the place of the bull," that is, the arena. See "Grandee" and "Hidalgo."

Plebs ("A herd of vulgar *plebs*—a Latin word." I. 1).— The common crowd; hence the term "plebeian."

Ploverleigh (S.).—The village where the scene of the opera is set. In the original production, the second Act took place in the Market Place. Later both Acts were at the exterior of Sir Marmaduke's mansion. This was obviously an improvement, for it enabled the Villagers to be discovered exactly as and where they fell unconscious in Act I.

Pocket Borough ("I was sent by a pocket borough into Parliament." Pin. 1).—A Parliamentary seat of which the nomination was largely in the hands of an individual. Electoral reform has long since done away with this form of patronage, though it exists still in the appointments to livings in the Established Church. The Queen of the Fairies (I.) has "a borough or two at my disposal."

Poets.—The poets mentioned in the operas are: Anacreon (P.I. 2); Horace (R. 1); William Morris (R. 1); Ovid (I. 1; P.I. 2; R. 1); Swinburne (R. 1); Tennyson (Pat. 1).

POINT, JACK (Y.).—A strolling jester, in love with his singing partner, Elsie Maynard.

POINTDEXTRE, SIR MARMADUKE (S.).—An elderly Baronet, father of Alexis. The name is derived from the heraldic term dexter point which is the top right-hand corner of the shield. As this is reckoned from its position on the breast, it is, to beholders, on the top left-hand corner.

Poltwhistle, Sir Clarence (Y.).—One of Henry VIII's Secretaries of State, who, in charging his cousin, Colonel Fairfax, with sorcery, hopes to succeed to his estates.

POOH-BAH (M.).—"Lord High Everything Else," that is, all the chief offices of state except that of the Lord High Executioner, which is held by Ko-Ko.

Pooh-Bah's offices.—The following are the offices mentioned as being held by Pooh-Bah: Archbishop of Titipu; Attorney-General; Chancellor of the Exchequer; Commander-in-Chief; Coroner; First Commissioner of Police; First Lord of the Treasury; Groom of the Back Stairs; Groom of the Second

Floor Front; Home Secretary; Judge Ordinary;
Leader of the Opposition; Lord Chamberlain;
Lord Chief Justice; Lord High Admiral; Lord
Mayor (acting); Lord Mayor (elect); Master of the
Buckhounds; Master of the Rolls; Paymaster-
General; Private Secretary; Privy Purse; Registrar;
and Solicitor.

Pops of Sillery ("And pops of Sillery our light artillery."
P.I. 1).—Sillery is a town on the River Marne
celebrated for its champagne. The young gallants,
therefore, intend to capture the fair undergraduates
of Castle Adamant by the popping of champagne
corks rather than of heavy guns.

PORTER, SIR JOSEPH, K.C.B. (Pin.).—First Lord of the
Admiralty. Abandoning his idea of marrying
Josephine when it is discovered that her father is
but a common sailor, he allies himself to his cousin
Hebe.

POUNDS, COURTICE.—Created the parts of
Colonel Fairfax in *The Yeomen of the Guard* and of
Marco in *The Gondoliers*. Appeared in the original
production of *The Mikado* as Nanki-Poo. He suc-
ceeded Durward Lely as principal tenor of the
company, and created several other parts at the
Savoy, including the juvenile lead in Grundy and
Sullivan's *Haddon Hall* and Dance and Solomon's
Nautch Girl. On leaving the Savoy, his greatest
successes were in *La Poupée* and *Chu Chin Chow*.

POWER, (SIR) GEORGE.—Created the parts of
Ralph in *Pinafore* and Frederic in *The Pirates of
Penzance*. Appeared in the original production of
The Sorcerer as Alexis. Later succeeded to his father's

baronetcy and became a well-known teacher of singing.

Precious Stones.—The following are the precious stones mentioned in the operas: diamond (Pat. 2; P.I. 1; G. 1); pearl (S. 2); ruby (T. by J.).

Preme (G. 2).—An Italian word, introduced in the last chorus of the opera, signifying "hurry up."

PRICE, S.—Created the part of Sir Rupert Murgatroyd the first Baronet of Ruddigore. Also appeared in the original production of *The Mikado* as Pish-Tush; and of *Ruddigore* as Sir Despard.

Primordial ("A . . . primordial atomic globule." M. 1). Primary, pertaining to first principles.

Princes.—The Princes in the operas are: Hilarion, Arac, Guron, and Scynthius (P.I.); Nanki-Poo (M.); and Monte Carlo (G.D.). Luiz (G.), although uncrowned, is already the King of Barataria.

Princesses.—The Princesses in the operas are: Ida (P.I.); Zara, Nekaya, and Kalyba (U.); and Monte Carlo (G.D.). Casilda (G.) is already a Queen, as she was married to Luiz when a baby.

PRINCESS IDA, or *CASTLE ADAMANT*.—The seventh opera. Produced at the Savoy Theatre, January 5, 1884, and ran till October 9, 1884, with a total of 147 performances. It was never revived during Mrs. D'Oyly Carte's tenure of the Savoy Theatre.

NOTES ON "PRINCESS IDA"

The work is styled by the author "a respectful perversion of Tennyson's *Princess*." It is also an

operatic version of Gilbert's *Princess*, produced at
the Olympic Theatre on January 8, 1870. The
characters are identical except for the omission
of Gobbo, the porter, the only male inmate of
Castle Adamant.

The libretto is written entirely in blank verse, of
heroic metre, that is, of ten-syllable lines.

The final lines—
    "We will walk the world
Yoked in all exercise of noble end!
And so through those dark gates across the wild
That no man knows!"
are taken verbatim from Tennyson's work.

The music to Gama's Song in Act III, "I've
nothing whatever to grumble at," was entirely
altered almost at the last moment, and Grossmith
had to unlearn the original, which he confessed was
one of the hardest things he ever had to do.

It was during the original run of this work that
the illustrated programmes were installed. See
"Havers, Alice."

Privy Purse (M. 1).—The Treasurer of the private
income of the monarch. This is an office, therefore,
which Pooh-Bah, as a local minister and personally
unknown to the Mikado, could scarcely have held.

Protoplasmal ("A protoplasmal . . . globule." M. 1).
—Pertaining to the lowest form of animal or vege-
table life. It is usually written "protoplasmic."

P

PSYCHE, LADY (P.I.).—Professor of the Humanities at Castle Adamant. See "Humanities." She is Florian's sister, and falls in love with Cyril.

Puling ("Tush, I am puling." S. 1 and 2).—Twice spoken by Dr. Daly. "Whimpering" or "childish whining."

Q

Quarter-deck ("A man who hails from the quarter-deck." Pin. 1).—That part of the upper deck abaft the mainmast. It is used as a promenade for officers.

Quatrain (Y. 1).—One of the kinds of verse with which Jack Point can "rhyme you." A stanza of four lines rhyming alternately.

QUEEN OF THE FAIRIES (I.).—She banished Iolanthe for marrying a mortal, but eventually falls a victim herself to the attractions of Private Willis.

"Queen to save her head should come a-suing" (Y. 1).—No Queen is recorded in history as having "sued to save her head" actually whilst in the Tower. But it probably refers to Anne Boleyn in 1536, in which case the story of the opera would be dated a year or two later. For further reference as to this date, see "Archbishop of Canterbury."

Queens.—The Queens in the operas are the Queen of the Fairies (I.) and the Queen of Barataria (G.). There is also a Queen-Elect, Lady Sophy (U.). Both Gama and Hildebrand (P.I.) are presumably widowers.

Queen's Bench (I. 1).—See "Exchequer."

Quip and Quiddity ("Give us quip and quiddity." Y. 1).—A quip is a taunt or gibe; a quiddity is a quibble or cavil.

R

Rackstraw, Ralph (Pin.).—Able Seaman, in love
with the Captain's daughter, Josephine. His Christian name is pronounced "Rafe."

RALLAND, HERBERT.—Created the part of Mr.
Blushington in *Utopia Limited*.

RAMSAY, MR.—Appeared in the original production
of *Pinafore* as Bob Becket.

Ranunculus bulbosus (P.I. 2).—A buttercup. This flower
not being a bulb plant, the more correct term is
ranunculus tuberosus.

Ravelin ("When I know what is meant by . . . ravelin."
Pir. 1).—A detached work with two embankments
which make a salient angle. (*Mil.*)

Rederring (R. 1).—The Cornish village which forms
the scene of Act I.

REDMOND, MR.—Created the part of the First
Citizen in *The Yeomen of the Guard*.

Regiments.—The Army regiments represented in the
operas are: Grenadier Guards: Alexis (S.) and
Private Willis (I.); Royal Marines: Sergeant and
Party (Pin.); Dragoon Guards: Calverley, Murga-
troyd, the Duke of Dunstable, and Squad (Pat.);
Life Guards: Fitzbattleaxe and four Troopers (U.).
The Yeomen of the Guard, headed by the Sergeant
(Y.) are a special corps, correctly dressed with
"H" on their tunics to represent Henry VIII. The
uniforms of the Chorus of Men in Act I of *Ruddigore*

128

represent various regiments as dressed in the Peninsular War. Stanley's regiment (Pir.) is not specified, while Frederic, although attired in Act II in the undress uniform of a Cavalry Officer, cannot possibly be in the Service.

The Army ranks are:—Major-General: Stanley (Pir.); Colonels: Calverley (Pat.) and Fairfax (Y.); Major: Murgatroyd (Pat.); Captain: Fitz-battleaxe (U.); Lieutenants: Alexis (presumably) (S.), and the Duke of Dunstable (Pat.); Sergeants: Of Marines (Pin.) and Meryll of the Yeomen of the Guard (Y.); Corporal: Of the Yeomen of the Guard (Y.); Troopers: Of the Dragoon Guards (Pin.) and of the Life Guards (U.); Privates: Of the Marines (Pin.) and Willis of the Grenadiers (I.). Pooh-Bah was Commander-in-Chief (M.).

Repente ("Of a sudden, which is English for *repente*." I. 1) (*It.*).—Sudden or unexpected.

Reversed in Banc (T. by J.).—The setting aside of the judgment of a Common Law Judge by a superior Court, such as a Full Court or a Court of Appeal.

Revising Barrister ("The Revising Barrister expunges his name." G.D. 1).—The official who is responsible for the list of voters at Parliamentary Elections.

Rhyme—the most frequent.—The two words which Gilbert utilizes as rhymes most frequently are "beauty" and "duty." There are fifteen instances, exclusive of repetitions, these being as follows:

1. *Trial by Jury.*
   "Time may do his duty;
   Winter hath a beauty."
                              Bridesmaids' Chorus.

2. *Sorcerer* (1).
   > "Some love for rank, and some for duty;
   > And others love for youth and beauty."
   > > Song. Alexis.

3. *Sorcerer* (2).
   > "No highborn exacting beauty
   > But a wife who'll do her duty."
   > > Sir Marmaduke in Quintet.

4. *Pinafore* (1).
   > "Our saucy ship's a beauty;
   > And attentive to our duty."
   > > Sailors' Chorus.

5. *Pinafore* (1).
   > "A bride of blushing beauty;
   > To do her menial's duty."
   > > Ballad. Ralph.

6. *Pinafore* (1).
   > "Unfeeling beauty,
   > It is my duty."
   > > Duet. Josephine and Ralph.

7. *Pinafore* (2).
   > "So peerless in his manly beauty
   > Were little else than solemn duty."
   > > Song. Josephine.

8. *Pirates* (1).
   > "Which does not feel the moral beauty
   > Subordinate to sense of duty."
   > > Song. Frederic.

9. *Pirates* (1).
   > "A thing of beauty,
   > A sense of duty."
   > > Girls' Chorus.

10. *Pirates* (1).
    "From dream of homely duty
    With such exceeding beauty."

    Solo. Mabel.

11. *Patience* (1).
    "That every beauty
    Will feel it her duty."

    Song. Colonel.

12. *Yeomen of the Guard* (1).
    "For conscience and for home in all its
    beauty;
    That comes not in the measure of its duty."
    Song. Dame Carruthers.

13. *Gondoliers* (1).
    "Two there are for whom in duty;
    Two so peerless in their beauty."

    Girls' Chorus.

14. *Utopia* (1).
    "His home and island beauty;
    —Of Regimental Duty."

    Duet. Zara and Fitzbattleaxe.

15. *Utopia* (1).
    "In charge of Youth and Beauty,
    As Regimental Duty."

    Duet. Zara and Fitzbattleaxe.

Rialto ("Scramble money on the Rialto." G. 1).—
The famous bridge across the Grand Canal, Venice,
built in 1588. It was formerly used as a kind of
open-air Exchange.

RICHARDS, MR.—Created the part of the Headsman in *The Yeomen of the Guard*. He was of imposing

stature, and his services were requisitioned for subsequent revivals.

Richardson's Show (Pat. 1).—Mentioned in the Colonel's Song. An interesting account of this travelling show is to be found in "Greenwich Fair," one of the chapters in Dickens's *Sketches by Boz.*

RICHMOND, BELLA.—Appeared in the original production of *The Sorcerer* as Constance.

Rival Admirers' Clauses Consolidation Act (U. 2). —The Act which Captain Fitzbattleaxe invents in order to pretend to hold Princess Zara in trust for Scaphio and Phantis, his rivals for her hand.

RIVIERA, DUKE OF (G.D. 2).—One of the pseudo-Peers in the suite of the Prince of Monte Carlo. Pronounced as a quadrasyllable: "Ree-vee-air-a."

Robinson Crusoe (G. 2).—Daniel Defoe's immortal hero. Mentioned in the Duke and Duchess's duet, "Robinson Crusoe would jib at their wearing apparel." The author is mentioned in Pat. 1.

Roddy-Doddy (R. 2).—Dame Hannah's pet name for her ghostly lover Sir Roderic.

"Rode a horse." (Pir. 1).—In the encore for the last verse of Major-General Stanley's Patter Song, he substitutes these words in mistake for "Sat a gee," the correct rhyme to "strategy."

Roderick ("Swagger of Roderick, heading his clan." Pat. 1).—From the Colonel's Song. It can refer either to the last of the Goths whose legendary history forms one of Scott's poems, or to the King of Ireland, crowned in 1166 and deposed in 1191.

Rondolet (Y. 1).—One of Jack Point's forms of rhyming. Originally "roundlet," a diminutive of "roundel," a round dance.

ROOSEVELT, BLANCHE.—Appeared in the original production of *Pinafore* as Josephine.

ROSE, ANNIE.—Appeared in the original production of *The Mikado* as Katisha.

ROSE, CHARLES R.—Created the part of Francesco in *The Gondoliers*. Appeared in the original production of *The Yeomen of the Guard* as Fairfax and Leonard, and of *The Gondoliers* as Marco, Luiz, and Giuseppe.

ROSE, JESSIE.—Created the part of Bertha in *The Grand Duke*. In the final series of revivals during Mrs. D'Oyly Carte's management, she was the chief soubrette, succeeding Florence Perry, who succeeded Jessie Bond. Her husband was Percy Elliott, for some years the leader of the Savoy orchestra.

Rosherville ("I spend the day at Rosherville." S. 2). Rosherville Gardens, near Gravesend, was a popular pleasaunce. Its attractions, however, gradually waned, and it ended by becoming the site of an oil factory. The significance of the above quotation is that Rosherville was extensively advertised as "the place to spend a happy day."

Rothschild.—The famous Anglo-German banking firm is mentioned (i) in the Lord Chancellor's Dream Song (I. 2), "Ever so many are taken by Rothschild . . . ," and (ii) in Mr. Goldbury's Song (U. 1), "Though a Rothschild you may be."

Roundelay ("This (joyous) (weary) roundelay." Pir. 2).—A short simple song with a refrain. Often the refrain itself.

ROWAN, MR.—Appeared in the original production of *Iolanthe* as Earl Tolloller.

Rowbottom, Little Ruth (R. 1).—One of the objects of Rose Maybud's charity.

ROWLEY, MINA.—Appeared in the original production of *Iolanthe* as Celia.

Royalty Theatre.—The birthplace of *Trial by Jury*. It is in Dean Street, Soho, and was rebuilt in 1882, since which date it has several times been renovated.

Rubicon ("Having crossed the Rubicon." G. 2).—A stream between Italy and Cisalpine Gaul, crossed by Julius Caesar in 49 B.C. Having once been crossed, it was almost impossible to return. Hence, the phrase means "to take the irrevocable step."

RUDDIGORE, or *THE WITCH'S CURSE*.—Ninth opera. Produced at the Savoy Theatre, January 22, 1887, and ran until November 5, 1887, with a total of 288 performances. It was never revived during Mrs. D'Oyly Carte's tenancy.

NOTES ON "RUDDIGORE"

The original title was intended to be "Kensington Gore" or "Robin and Richard were two pretty men." It was altered to *Ruddygore* on its production, and, on February 2nd, to its final title.

———

The coming to life of the pictures was taken from Gilbert's early work, *Ages Ago*.

———

The costumes were extremely expensive. Some of the uniforms cost £150 each, and five hundred pounds' worth of costumes was discarded as they were found to resemble those worn in the Gaiety burlesque *Monte Cristo Junior*.

At the first performances, Sir Roderic rose through a trap-door, but, later, the better course was adopted of making him come, like the others, from his picture-frame. All the pictures were exact representations of the actors who played the parts when coming to life.

During the run, (Sir) Henry Lytton made his first appearance at the Savoy on February 2nd. Grossmith was away and remained absent, owing to illness, for about a fortnight. The part of Robin Oakapple was taken by Lytton, who appeared under the name of H. Henri. His adopted name is significant. He was married to Louie Henri (now Lady Lytton), who was a principal in the touring company. But, owing to his youth, he originally posed as her brother. Miss Henri herself appeared at the Savoy as Tessa in a later revival of *The Gondoliers*.

On April 5, Leonora Braham bade farewell to the Savoy Theatre Company.

The Finale of Act II has been altered since the original production. The final chorus, "Having been a wicked baronet a week," which, strangely enough, did not appear before in the opera, is now omitted. It did, however, appear in the original

Overture, which has now been superseded by a new one arranged by Geoffrey Toye.

Ruddigore Castle (R. 2).—The Scene of Act II, depicting the Picture Gallery.

RUDOLPH (G.D.).—Grand Duke of Pfennig-Halbpfennig, whose matrimonial complications, sustained by his substitute Ludwig, form the plot of the opera. See "Pfennig-Halbpfennig."

Rule the roast ("Wouldn't you like to rule the roast?" P.I. 2).—To be head of affairs. The expression is used by Shakespeare: "The new-made duke that rules the roast."

Rumbelow ("With a yeo heave ho and a rumbelow." M. 1).—A meaningless combination of syllables used as a sailors' refrain when rowing.

RUSSELL, SCOTT.—Created the parts of Lord Dramaleigh in *Utopia Ltd.* and of the Notary in *The Grand Duke*. Subsequently he was associated with Sir Nigel Playfair's productions at the Lyric, Hammersmith, and is almost the only creator of Gilbert and Sullivan parts still playing, at the time of writing.

RUTH (i) (Pir.).—Pirate Maid of all Work, in love with the apprentice Frederic, her former charge when a nursery maid. Disappointed in her desire to secure him, she subsequently allies herself to the Sergeant of Police.

(ii) (R.).—The second leader of the Professional Bridesmaids.

Ruthven (R.).—The real Christian name of Robin Oakapple. Pronounced in this opera precisely as spelt. See "Elision."

RYLEY, CHARLES.—Created the part of Florian in *Princess Ida*. Appeared in the original production of *Iolanthe* as Private Willis.

SACHARISSA (P.I.).—One of the Girl Graduates. She is expelled for possessing a set of chess-men, but is reinstated when war is declared, becoming the Lady Surgeon.

Sacheverell, Dr. (Pat. 1).—Mentioned in the Colonel's Song. A High Church clergyman who was tried at Westminster Hall for having preached a violent sermon at St. Paul's on Guy Fawkes' Day, 1709. He was acquitted, and later became Rector of St. Andrew's, Holborn. The name is pronounced with the accent on the second syllable.

Sailors.—The only naval man mentioned in the operas is: Nelson (Pat. 1; R. 1).

SALATA (U.).—One of the Utopian maidens.

Salisbury Plain ("Crossing Salisbury Plain on a bicycle." I. 2).—From the Lord Chancellor's Dream Song.

Sally Lunn ("Now for the gay Sally Lunn." S. 1).—So called from a girl of that name, who sold such tea-cakes in the streets of Bath at the beginning of the nineteenth century.

SAMUEL (Pir.).—The Pirate King's Lieutenant, who ultimately allies himself to the Major-General's daughter Kate.

SANGAZURE, LADY (S.).—A lady of ancient lineage and mother of Aline. The word means "Blue blood." This is the only principal part in any of the operas (except *Trial by Jury*, which has no dialogue) which has no spoken word.

SAPHIR, THE LADY (Pat.).—One of the chief Rapturous Maidens, who allies herself to Colonel Calverley. See "Angela, The Lady."

Saraband (Y. 1).—One of Jack Point's dances. A slow, stately measure in triple time. Shakespeare describes it as "a measure full of state and ancientry." The Italian form is more modern than that of the Spanish, which is quicker and danced with castanets.

SAUMAREZ, CISSIE.—Appeared in the original production of *The Gondoliers* as Gianetta, Tessa, Casilda, and Fiametta. She became the wife of Arthur Whitby, the actor.

Savoy Hotel.—The famous hotel adjoining and connecting the Savoy Theatre was opened nearly eight years after the theatre, on August 6, 1889. It was intended largely to be a convenient place to dine before the performance, and much of the business management of the D'Oyly Carte Company is done there. The original Directors were the Earl of Lathom, Sir Arthur Sullivan, Mr. D'Oyly Carte, and Mr. Hwfa Williams.

Savoy Theatre.—Opened October 10, 1881. It was bounded by Beaufort Buildings, Somerset Street, Carting Lane, and Herbert's Passage. It shared with the Criterion Theatre the distinction of having the auditorium below the level of the street, and exit could be made from all four sides. It was the first to have the following features:—An Act Drop divided at the centre and drawn by being caught up to the wings; the Swan incandescent burner; the no-fee system; free programmes; prohibition of gratuities; and an organized queue. The architect was C. J. Phipps; the builders, Patman and Fotheringham; the painters, Collinson and Lock; the upholsterers, Wadman & Co.; the marble vestibule makers, Burke & Co.; the concrete floor suppliers, Drake & Co.; the electricians, Faraday & Son; the fire appliance providers, Messrs. Merryweather; iron shutter makers, Clarke & Co. The run of *Patience* was transferred from the Opera Comique on the opening night, and *Iolanthe* was the first opera to be produced at the Savoy, although every one of the series has been performed there. The theatre held 1,292 persons, with 6 boxes, 150 stalls, 160 dress circle, 200 pit and 500 balcony and gallery. It has twice been rebuilt and altered.

SCAPHIO (U.).—One of the Judges of the Utopian Supreme Court, who, with Phantis the other, controls the King's actions.

SCHUBERTH, ANNIE.—A well-known American artist who appeared in the original production of *The Gondoliers* as Gianetta.

SCYNTHIUS (P.I.).—One of King Gama's three sons.

Selvagee ("I can . . . ship a selvagee." Pin. 1).—A skein of rope-yarns wound round with marline, used for stoppers or straps. (*Naut.*)

Senex Senior (U. 1).—The pseudonym adopted, under compulsion, by the King for his article, "How long is this to last?" in the *Palace Peeper*.

SERGEANT OF MARINES (Pin.).—He and his party go through the formality of presenting arms continually during the First Lord's opening song. He also attends to Ralph Rackstraw's arrest in Act II.

SERGEANT OF POLICE (Pir. 2).—The leader of the posse of policemen detailed to subdue and arrest the Pirates. He subsequently allies himself to Ruth.

Servitors ("You'll find no . . . servitors here." P.I. 2). —Poor undergraduates at Oxford, who had to wait at table.

"Set us free" (S. 1).—Sprites expected to be granted their freedom after performing some important task for their masters. Compare Ariel's request in Shakespeare's *Tempest*.

Seven bells ("At Seven Bells." Pin. 1).—At "Seven Bells" all hands are called aft in the Navy. A watch is four hours, and each bell represents a half-hour. Seven bells would therefore mean a half-hour before the end of a watch.

Seven Dials (I. 1.)—Seven narrow streets converging on St. Martin's Lane, near Charing Cross. Now a respectable district, it formerly was a by-word for poverty, dirt, and crime.

Sewell and Cross ("A Sewell and Cross young man." Pat. 2).—A firm of drapers whose establishment was at the junction of Old Compton Street and Frith Street, Soho.

SEYMOUR, W. H.—Appeared in the original (London) production of *The Pirates of Penzance*.

Later he became Stage Manager to the Company, acting in that capacity up to the last opera, *The Grand Duke*.

SHADBOLT, WILFRED (Y.).—Head Jailer and Assistant Tormentor at the Tower of London, in love with Phoebe Meryll, who accepts his hand because "there is no help for it."

"Shalloo humps" and "Shalloo hoops." (G. 2).—From Giuseppe's song. Referring to the cryptic orders of the Sergeant on parade, these being the version of "shoulder arms" or "slope arms."

SHIRLEY, ELLEN.—Appeared in the original (London) production of *The Pirates of Penzance* as Mabel, and of *Patience* as Patience.

SHIRLEY, W. R.—Created the part of Leonard Meryll in *The Yeomen of the Guard*. Also appeared in the original production of *The Gondoliers* as Marco and Francesco.

Silk Purses ("Silk purses with their rigs." P.I. 2).—The original proverb, from Ray's Collection, is "You cannot make velvet out of a sow's ear."

Similar Character-Names.—The following are the similar character-names in the operas: Zorah: Mrs. Partlet (S.) and First Professional Bridesmaid (R.). Corcoran: Captain (Pin.) and Sir Edward (U.). Murgatroyd: Major (Pir.) and the Baronets of Ruddigore (R.). Ruth: Maid of all Work (Pir.) and Second Professional Bridesmaid (R.). Kate: Major-General Stanley's daughter (Pir.) and Dame Carruthers' niece (Y.). Richard: Richard Dauntless (R.) and Sir Richard Cholmondeley (Y.). Also the following similar Christian names of different countries: George: Earl Tolloller (I.) and Giorgio (G.). Joseph: Sir Joseph Porter (Pin.) and Giuseppe (G.). Julia: Giulia (G.) and Julia Jellicoe (G.D.). Elsie: Elsie Maynard (Y.) and Elsa (G.D.).

Sixes and Sevens ("Either at sixes or at sevens." Pin. 2).—This expression originates from a passage in Middleton's play, *The Widow*, Act I, Scene 2.

Sizars ("You'll find no sizars here." P.I. 2).—A sizar is at the Universities of Cambridge and Dublin what a servitor is at Oxford. See "Servitor."

Sloane Square ("Sloane Square and South Kensington stations." I. 2).—Gilbert's date for the story of the opera (1700–1882) can be narrowed down considerably, for these stations were opened in the late 1860's and early 1870's. Another indication is the reference to Captain Shaw, the Chief of the London Fire Brigade (*q.v.*).

Slyboots (Y. 1).—A humorous term for a saucily sly person. It is used by Goldsmith: "Slyboots was cursedly cunning."

Snickersee ("I drew my snickersee." M. 2).—A long knife, originating from the Dutch.

SNYDER, LEONORE.—Appeared in the original production of *The Gondoliers* as Gianetta. Later made a success in the leading part of George Dance and Edward Solomon's *Nautch Girl*, at the Savoy Theatre.

Sodor and Man, Bishop of ("Style of the Bishop of Sodor and Man." Pat. 1).—From the Colonel's Song. The official title of the Bishop of the Hebrides and the Isle of Man. Sodor is the old name for the Southern Islands, the Hebrides.

Soldiers.—The soldiers mentioned in the operas are: Caesar (Pat. 1); Caractacus (Pir. 1); Sir Richard Cholmondeley (Y.); Hannibal (Pat. 1); Roderick (Pat. 1); Lord Waterford (Pat. 1); Wellington (I. 2); and Wolseley (Pat. 1).

SOLICITOR, MR. BUNTHORNE's (Pat.).—He appears in Act I to arrange Bunthorne's raffle of himself. He does not speak, but alternately shows pleasure at the attention bestowed on him by the Rapturous Maidens, and alarm at the threatening attitude of the Dragoon Guards.

Somerset House ("A Somerset House young man." Pat. 2).—Somerset House, built by the Lord Protector Somerset, in the reign of Edward VI, chiefly from masonry salved from old St. Paul's, is now the place of depository for proved wills and for documents relating to Inland Revenue, etc.

SOPHY, THE LADY (U.).—The English *gouvernante* of the young Utopian Princesses. She eventually becomes Queen-Elect of Utopia.

SORCERER, THE.—Second opera. Produced at the Opera Comique, November 17, 1877. It ran till May 24, 1878, with a total of 175 performances. It was revived in 1884 and 1898, the aggregate number of performances being 327.

S

NOTES ON "THE SORCERER"

During the original run, *Trial by Jury* was revived, in which Grossmith played the Judge. This is mentioned because it is thought by some that Grossmith never played in the first work.

———

Mr. Wells's "business" with the teapot is a burlesque of the Incantation Scene from Weber's *Der Freischütz*.

———

On March 9, 1878, the touring company played *The Sorcerer* at the matinée. Amongst the cast was Rosina Brandram, who played Lady Sangazure.

———

In the original production Dr. Daly had curly hair and a moustache.

———

There is no reason why Dr. Daly should fall in love with Aline. Those who drank the love-potion fell in love with the first person of the opposite sex encountered. The Vicar has already seen all the village maidens.

———

In one of the post-war revivals the Dance by the Villagers at the commencement of Act II was done to the music of the Country Dance from Act I of Sydney Grundy and Arthur Sullivan's *Haddon Hall*.

Soupçon ("Just a soupçon of this sort of thing." G. 2) (*Fr.*).—Suspicion. The "p" should be silent, the pronunciation being, approximately ,"soossong."

South Kensington ("Oh, South Kensington." Pat. 1). —The signification of Lady Jane's ejaculation is doubtful. It may refer (i) to the Arts side of South Kensington Museum, (ii) to the fact that South Kensington was a district where aestheticism flourished, (iii) to the Royal School of Art where, in the 80's, needlework of crude colours was affected by ladies in reduced circumstances, (iv) to the propinquity to the Guards' Barracks, where, as is evidenced by the Dragoon Guards, the uniforms were mainly red and yellow.

Spaniard from Arragon ("The family pride of a Spaniard from Arragon." Pat. 1).—From the Colonel's Song. The correct spelling is Aragon. The Aragonese are a particularly haughty race.

Speisesaal (G.D. 1).—The town where, in the Market Place, the first Act is set. The word means a dining hall. (*Ger.*)

"Spoils the rod who spares the child" (Pin. 2).—The usual version "Spare the rod and spoil the child" is from Samuel Butler's *Hudibras*, Part II, Canto I, but this is derived from "He that spareth the rod hateth his son" (Proverbs xiii. 24).

Sposo ("Am I quite the gallant *sposo*?" G.D. 1).— Spouse, husband. (*It.*)

SQUIRE, EMILY.—Appeared in the original production of *The Gondoliers* as Gianetta.

Stali (G. 2).—From the concluding chorus of the opera. A word used by Venetian gondoliers and others, meaning "Stop" or "Stay there."

STANLEY, MAJOR-GENERAL (Pir.).—The father of a number of marriageable daughters, who tells the "terrible story" that he is an orphan to save himself from the pirates.

St. James's Park ("She'll meet him after dark inside St. James's Park." I. 1).—What Tolloller thinks Iolanthe says to Strephon.

St. Mary Axe ("Number seventy, Simmery Axe." S.1). —A street leading into Leadenhall Street, wherein are the offices of John Wellington Wells & Co., Family Sorcerers.

STELLA, MLLE.—Appeared in the original production of *Trial by Jury* as the Plaintiff.

"Storks turn out to be but logs." (Pin. 2).—From Aesop's Fable of King Log and King Stork.

Strand Theatre.—At this theatre, the third series of the original production of *Trial by Jury* took place. See "Clarke, J. S."

Stranger ("The Stranger, a touch of him." Pat. 1).— From the Colonel's Song. Count Waldbourg, who, leaving his wife, roamed about the world and was known as the Stranger. He subsequently met his wife unexpectedly and was reconciled. He is the subject of a play by Kotzebue.

STREPHON (I.).—An Arcadian Shepherd in love with Phyllis. The name is borrowed from Sir Philip Sidney's *Arcadia*, but in that work Strephon's inamorata was Urania.

Subpoena ("Summoned by a stern subpoena." T. by J.). —Literally "under (threat of) punishment." Usually termed "writ," when applying to the summoning of a defendant to appear in court, subpoena generally referring to the summoning of a witness.

SULLIVAN, SIR ARTHUR SEYMOUR.—Born at 8, Boswell Terrace, Lambeth Walk, London, S.E., on May 13, 1842. The son of an Irish orchestral player and an Italian lady. From a choir boy at the Chapel Royal, he entered the Royal Academy of Music, where he won the Mendelssohn Scholarship, the second on the list being (Sir) Joseph Barnby, later Music Master at Eton College, and first conductor of the Royal Choral Society. He completed his musical education at Leipzig, and, on his return, conducted, in 1861, his first important work, the Incidental Music to *The Tempest*. His first light opera was *Contrabandista*, written to the libretto of (Sir) Francis Burnand, later the Editor of *Punch*, which was produced at the Savoy Theatre under the name of *The Chieftain* in 1898. He was knighted (together with Sir George Grove) on the occasion of the opening of the Royal College of Music in 1883, where he was a professor. He died on November 22, 1900.

SULLIVAN, FRED.—Sir Arthur Sullivan's brother, who created the part of the Learned Judge in *Trial by Jury*, dying during the run. He also appeared in *Thespis* (*q.v.*).

"Sunbeams from cucumbers" P.I. 2).—Suggested by Dean Swift's story of the Laputae, in *Gulliver's Travels*, who had spent eight years in an endeavour to extract sunbeams from cucumbers.

Swan and Edgar ("Let Swan secede from Edgar." P.I. 2).—The famous drapers at the corner of Regent Street and Piccadilly.

Swears and Wells ("We're Swears and Wells young girls." Pat. 2).—A famous firm of furriers and costumiers in Regent Street. They are now, under different management, in Oxford Street and Old Bailey.

Sweets, confectionery, etc.—The following sweets and confectionery are mentioned in the operas: butterscotch (G.D. 1); hardbake (G.D. 1); jujube (G.D. 1); peppermint drop (Pin. 1); peppermint rock (R. 1); sugar-plum (G. 2); and toffee (Pin. 1; Pat. 1).

Swinburne ("From Ovid and Horace to Swinburne and Morris." R. 1).—Algernon Charles Swinburne, the author of *Atalanta in Calydon*, and other poetical works. He lived for some time with his fellow-poet, Morris. See "Grosvenor Gallery."

SWORD BEARER (M.).—The small boy who carries Koko's Sword of State on his first entry.

Syllogistic ("reduced to syllogistic form." R. 2).— Pertaining to that kind of reasoning which consists of two premises and a conclusion. Thus the syllogism suggested is, "If forging a will is a crime and if a man can forge his own will (as he can do what he likes with his own), then forging one's own will is a crime."

T

"Take a maiden tender" (Pir. 1).—Ruth is not referring to herself, but is comparing the value of a love of but seventeen years' growth with that accumulated in forty-seven years.

TANNHÄUSER, DR. (G.D.).—A Notary who explains to the interested parties the nature of the Statutory Duel.

TARARA (U.).—The Public Exploder who conspires with the Judges, Scaphio and Phantis, to overthrow British influence in Utopia.

TAYLOR, J. G.—Appeared in the original production of *Trial by Jury* as the Judge. He also appeared in *Thespis*" (*q.v.*).

"Teaching pigs to fly" (P.I. 2).—The proverb is of comparatively modern date (1860), and runs, "Pigs may fly, but they are very unlikely birds."

Telephone ("No telephone communicates with his cell." Pin. 2).—Gilbert was up-to-date in this line, for the first Telephone Company in the City was founded in June 1878, and the first Telephone Exchange in August 1879.

TEMPLE, GEORGE.—Created the part of Samuel in *The Pirates of Penzance* (London). Also appeared in the original production of *The Gondoliers* as the Duke of Plaza-Toro, thus renewing his association with the London company after a lapse of ten years.

TEMPLE, RICHARD.—Created the parts of Sir Marmaduke Pointdextre in *The Sorcerer*; Dick Deadeye in *Pinafore*; the Pirate King in *The Pirates of Penzance*; Colonel Calverley in *Patience*; Strephon in *Iolanthe*; Arac in *Princess Ida*; the Mikado in *The Mikado*; Sir Roderic Murgatroyd in *Ruddigore*; and Sergeant Meryll in *The Yeomen of the Guard*. He declined the part of Antonio in *The Gondoliers*, but returned later to renew his parts in some of the revivals. He was in his latter years operatic trainer and producer at Trinity College of Music.

Tennyson (Pat. 1).—Mentioned in the Colonel's Song. Alfred, Lord Tennyson was Poet Laureate from 1840 until his death in 1892, at the age of eighty-three. Gilbert had particular reason to remember him, as his *Princess* was the original source of *Princess Ida*.

Tenterhooks ("Please do not keep us all on tenter hooks." G.D. 1).—This curious metaphor first appeared in Samuel Butler's *Hudibras*. A tenter hook is a sharp hooked nail used for fastening cloth on a frame for drying purposes.

Ten years ago ("Why didn't we marry ten years ago?" G. 1).—Marco is here indulging in a mere figure of speech, for he could not then have been more than ten or eleven years old, as he was an infant twenty years ago.

Tessa (G.).—One of the two principal Contadine, married to Giuseppe.

Tetrapods ("Tetrapods tragical." S. 1).—Insects with four legs, such as butterflies, or four-legged tables.

Thackeray ("Narrative powers of . . . Thackeray." Pat. 1).—From the Colonel's Song. The famous author of *Vanity Fair* and *Henry Esmond* was born in 1811, and died in 1863.

THESPIS, or *THE GODS GROWN OLD*.—Gilbert and Sullivan's first work. Produced at the Gaiety Theatre, December 26, 1871, under the management of John Hollingshead. Thespis is the manager of a theatrical company which visits Mount Olympus, where the deities are found to be greatly degenerated. The latter, desiring to visit the Earth, deputize their functions to the players, each taking the place of one or other of the gods and goddesses. They make a fearful hash of things, and, on the gods' return, are ignominiously ejected. The very strong cast included J. L. Toole as Thespis, Nelly Farren as Mercury, and two who subsequently appeared under D'Oyly Carte, Fred. Sullivan and J. G. Taylor. The work was never published, and, indeed, formed but a portion of the Gaiety entertainment.

Thomas (I. 2).—The Christian name of Earl Tolloller.

THORNTON, FRANK.—Created the part of Major Murgatroyd in *Patience*. Also appeared in the original production of *Pinafore* as Dick Deadeye; of *The Pirates of Penzance* (London) as Major-General Stanley; and of *Patience* as Bunthorne. He played the chief comedian parts on tour for a long time, but returned to the Savoy Theatre in 1892 to take a leading part in *The Nautch Girl*.

"Ties pay the dealer" (I. 2).—From the Lord Chancellor's Dream Song. In certain card games, if the cards held by the banker, who is also the dealer, are of equal value to those of another player, the banker wins.

Tiled. ("We are all tiled here." G.D. 1).—A Masonic expression, meaning to be free from intrusion by outsiders. It may be considered here as meaning "We are all initiated in a secret society."

Timoneer ("the trade of a timoneer." G. 1).—A helmsman.

Titipu (M.).—The town where the story of the opera takes place.

Titled Characters (British).—The following are the persons of title in the operas:—Duke: Dunstable (Pat). Peers of unknown rank: Pirate King and all the Pirates (Pir.); Lord Chancellor and the Peers' chorus (I.); Lord Dramaleigh (U.). Earls: Mountararat and Tolloller (I.). Peeresses: Iolanthe and in Act II all the Fairies (I.). Peers' (or Baronets' or Knights') widows, presumably: Lady Sangazure (S.); Lady Blanche (P.I.). Peers' Daughters: Jane, Angela, Saphir, and Ella (Pat.); Psyche (P.I.); Sophy (U.). Baronets: Sir Marmaduke Pointdextre (S.); Robin Oakapple and all the Ancestors (R.) Knights: the Learned Judge (presumably) (T. by J.); Sir Joseph Porter (Pin.); Sir Richard Cholmondeley (Y.); Sir Edward Corcoran and Sir Bailey Barre (U.). Those in M. are Japanese; in G., Spanish; in G.D., German. Mad Margaret (R.) in Act II is merely Mrs. Despard Murgatroyd.

Titled Savoyards.—In addition to Sir William Gilbert and Sir Arthur Sullivan, two Savoyards have borne titles whilst actively engaged in the operas, the Countess von Klinsky (Ilka von Palmay) the Julia Jellicoe of *The Grand Duke*; and Sir Henry Lytton. Two others became titled people after leaving the Savoy: George Power, later Sir George Power, Bart.; and Decima Moore, later Lady Guggisberg. Mention must also be made to the wife of Mr. Rupert D'Oyly Carte, Lady Dorothy.

Toco (M. 1).—Derived from the Greek, meaning chastisement. It appears first in Bee's *Dictionary of the Turf*, 1823.

Tocsin ("Though the tocsin sounds, ere long." M. 2). —A public alarm bell, used generally as a call to arms, or to arouse citizens in cases of public danger or emergency.

TOLLOLLER, EARL (I.).—One of the two noble lords who are temporarily engaged to Phyllis.

Tommy ("Soft tommy." Pin. 1).—Soft bread, meaning, generally, new rolls.

Tomtit (R. 1).—The Revenue Sloop of which Richard Dauntless was one of the crew.

Tontine Principle (U. 1).—So-called from its inventor, Tonti, a seventeenth-century Italian. Loans to the State, which may be described as a lottery of annuities or compound of lottery and annuity under which the subscribers who live longest receive the whole income of the annuities created by way of interest on the loans. The system has not been used in England for public loans since 1789, but Tontine Clubs in aid of private adventures have at times been constituted, and appear not to fall within the Acts against gaming. See the *Encyclopaedia of the Laws of England*, vol. xii. With regard to the reference to the Tontine principle in U. 1, Fitzbattleaxe, being quite a young man, expects to benefit by it, the "annuity" being no less than the hand of Princess Zara, the other prospective beneficiaries of the "lottery," Scaphio and Phantis, being sixty-six and fifty-five years of age respectively.

Total Performances.—The total performances of the Gilbert and Sullivan operas from the opening night of *Trial by Jury* to the closing night of Mrs. D'Oyly Carte's tenure of the Savoy Theatre in 1909 (exclusive of those given by children, by the touring companies, and by the opposition company at the Olympic Theatre) were as follows: *Mikado*, 1,183; *Pinafore*, 918; *Gondoliers*, 789; *Patience*, 779; *Yeomen of the Guard*, 699; *Pirates*, 616; *Trial by Jury*, 606; *Iolanthe*, 593; *Sorcerer*, 327; *Ruddigore*, 288; *Utopia*, 245; *Princess Ida*, 147; and *Grand Duke*, 123. Grand total, 7,606.

Tower from the Wharf (Y. 2).—This was the scene of Act II in the revival of 1897, but since then it has remained the same as Act. I.

Tower Green ("A worthy . . . gentleman is to be beheaded . . . on this very spot." Y. 1).—This is a concession to the exigencies of the stage. Worthy gentlemen were not executed on Tower Green, but on Tower Hill, without the precincts. Only Exalted Personages had the doubtful privilege of being beheaded on Tower Green, with the additional distinction of being interred in S. Peter ad Vincula. Six persons in all suffered here, these being Queen Anne Boleyn, Queen Katherine Howard, Lady Jane Grey, the Earl of Essex, the Viscountess Rochford, and the Countess of Salisbury. Even Lady Jane's husband, Dudley, was refused the privilege.

Transmutations ("What transmutations have been conjured by the silent alchemy of twenty years." P.I. 1).—A poetical metaphor, likening the change which years bring about to the attempts of alchemists to discover the philosopher's stone, i.e. the conversion of base metal into gold.

Trap-doors.—Stage trap-doors are necessary only in two of the operas. Iolanthe rises from the stream (I. 1), and John Wellington Wells descends to Ahrimanes (S. 2). There was, however, another instance, abandoned after the first few performances. Sir Roderic Murgatroyd rose from a trapdoor into the Picture Gallery (R. 2).

Trees.—The following trees are mentioned in the operas: bay (G.D. 2); ivy (G.D. 2); oak (P.I. 2; R. 2); and poplar (Pir. 2; U. 2).

Tremorden Castle (Pir. 2).—Major-General Stanley's newly acquired estate, of which the ruined chapel forms the scene of Act II.

Trepan ("Weazels at their slumbers they trepan." P.I. 2).—Used here in the less usual sense of "ensnare," the word "trepan" more generally being associated with an operation on the skull. The accomplishment of the Girl Graduates suggested here is a converse of the saying, "You can never catch a weazel asleep."

τρέπεσθαι πρòς τòν πότον (G.D. 2) (*Gr.*).—Pronounced "tre-pess-thy pross ton potton." To take to drinking. The expression is found in Plato.

TREVOR, MR.—Created the part of the 6th Baronet, Sir Lionel Murgatroyd, in *Ruddigore*.

TRIAL BY JURY.—The first opera. In one Act, and styled originally a Dramatic Cantata. Its first production was in three periods with a few weeks between each. It was first given at the Royalty Theatre on March 25, 1875, under the management of Seline Dolaro (*q.v.*) and D'Oyly Carte; then at the Opera Comique under Charles Morton (*q.v.*), and lastly at the Strand Theatre under John S. Clarke (*q.v.*). The total of these combined performances was 294. It was revived in 1879, 1884, and 1898, the total aggregate of performances being 606.

NOTES ON "TRIAL BY JURY"

Shortly after the original production there was a series of Recital Performances at the Royal Aquarium. These are not reckoned in the number of official performances. They were specially notable for the appearance amongst the cast of two artists, widely distinct in their style, but equally famous in their own sphere: Madame Mary Davies, the eminent soprano, and James Fawn, the music-hall comedian.

―――――

The cast during the original run was constantly changed, and at the final performance only one original member remained, W. S. Penley, later of *The Private Secretary* and *Charley's Aunt* fame. He had at various times taken the parts of the Judge, the Usher, and the Foreman.

―――――

At the Finale of the first performances red fire was burnt and a couple of plaster Cupids descended on the Plaintiff and the Judge.

―――――

At the 1884 revival, there was a kind of Harlequinade, with the Judge as Harlequin, the Plaintiff as Columbine, and the Bridesmaids as Counsel in wig and gown.

Trice ("I can prove it in a trice." G. 2).—This term, meaning immediately, is derived from the Spanish *tris*, the sound of the sudden breaking of glass. It is used by Shakespeare.

Triolet ("Oh, dainty triolet." P.I. 1).—This is merely a convenient rhyme to "violet" and has no significance here. A triolet is a poem of eight lines, in which the first line is repeated at the fourth and seventh lines.

Trollope, Anthony (Pat. 1).—Mentioned in the Colonel's Song. The distinguished novelist was born in 1815, and died on the last evening of the original run of *Patience*, in 1882. His best-known works are *Doctor Thorne*, *Barchester Towers*, and *Orley Farm*.

Trusty (R. 2).—Dame Hannah's surname, her father being Stephen Trusty.

"Truth is always strong" (P.I. 2).—A misquotation of "Truth is always strange," from Byron's *Don Juan*.

Tucker, Tommy (Pin.).—The small midshipman on board the *Pinafore*. Though he does not speak, he has several bits of "business," such as accepting a sugarstick from Little Buttercup, and shaking hands with the Boatswain's Mate during "He is an Englishman."

Tuer, Mr.—Created the part of the 16th Baronet, Sir Desmond Murgatroyd, in *Ruddigore*.

Tufts ("You'll find no tufts to mark nobility." P.I. 2).
—In bygone days at the Universities, young noble
undergraduates used to wear gold tufts on their
college caps to distinguish them from commoners.

Tuppenny ("to tuck in his tuppenny." G. 2).—A
slang expression for "head."

Tupper (Pat. 1).—Mentioned in the Colonel's Song.
Martin Tupper was a British author whose *Pro-
verbial Philosophy*, written in 1838, had the pheno-
menal sale of nearly two million copies. He died,
aged seventy-nine, in 1889.

Turkish Stock (S. 1).—In the original performance of
The Sorcerer, this was the "rise" mentioned by John
Wellington Wells, subsequently altered to "Unified."

Twelve hours (S. 1).—The time which it took for the
love-potion to operate. This being so, Aline would
not have fallen in love with Dr. Daly, practically
at sight.

Twelve o'clock ("You are one of us until the clock
strikes twelve." Pir. 1).—This refers to the custom
of apprentices being "out of their indentures" at
midday on the appointed day.

"Two strings to every bow" (I. 2).—This expression
is in Wolsey's State Papers of Henry VIII.

TWYNAM, MISS.—Created the part of Ada in
Princess Ida.

U

ULMAR, GERALDINE.—Created the parts of Elsie Maynard in *The Yeomen of the Guard* and Gianetta in *The Gondoliers*. Also appeared in the original production of *Ruddigore* as Rose Maybud. She married Ivan Caryll (Felix Tilkins), and later Jack Thompson, the song writer. She subsequently played many parts in other theatres, notably the title-role in *La Cigale*.

Unannealed ("Is he to die . . . unannealed?" Pir. 2).—Obsolete form of (un) "anele," which means to perform the religious rite of Extreme Unction. The word occurs also in P.I. 3.

Unified ("A rise in Unified." S. 1).—The Unified Debt Stock was a former name for Consols. There are also Egyptian Unified bonds still in existence. See "Turkish Stock."

Unshriven ("Is he to die unshriven?" Pir. 2).—To make aural confession and to receive absolution at the hands of a priest.

Usher (T. by J.).—His chief work in the opera is to see that the Jury are sworn, to summon Angelina into Court, to bring a glass of water to the Judge, and to convey amorous messages from his Lordship to the First Bridesmaid and the Plaintiff.

Utility ("We're wasted on "utility." U. 1).—A stage expression, meaning the player of any kind of subsidiary role which the particular play offers. Also such a part itself.

UTOPIA LTD., or *THE FLOWERS OF PRO-GRESS*.—Twelfth opera. Produced at the Savoy Theatre, October 7, 1893, and ran until June 9, 1894, with a total of 245 performances. It was never revived.

NOTES ON "UTOPIA LTD."

The original cast saw an almost total change of personnel, which may be said to form the company for the first series of revivals. This included Charles Kenningham, succeeding Courtice Pounds; Walter Passmore, the first great successor to George Grossmith; Scott Fishe; Emmie Owen; and Florence Perry, succeeding Jessie Bond. Only Rutland Barrington, Rosina Brandram, and W. H. Denny of the originals remained. Nancy McIntosh, who played the leading part, was Gilbert's adopted daughter. John Le Hay had not been seen in Savoy Opera since the Paignton production of *The Pirates of Penzance* in 1880.

———

Sir Edward Corcoran is introduced to the tune of "I am the Captain of the *Pinafore*." This was received with great rapture by the audience. Sir Edward, however, cannot be regarded as the quondam Captain, for the latter turned out to be merely an A.B.

———

This is the only opera which has for its Finale of Act II a number of which the music has not previously occurred.

V

Valley-de-Sham (R. 2).—Old Adam's pronunciation of *valet de chambre*.

Vapours ("Down in the mouth with the vapours." G.D. 1).—An old term for hypochondria. It is used by Pope.

VENNE, LOTTIE.—Appeared in the original production of *Trial by Jury* as the Plaintiff. Later, quitting the musical stage for straight plays, she became one of the finest comedy actresses in London.

Verbum sat. ("You mean, of course, by duel") (*verbum sat.*) (G.D.).—An abbreviation of "*verbum satis sapienti.*" "A word to the wise man is sufficient." It is often given as "*verb. sap.*"

Vernal ("O'er the season vernal." T. by J.).—Pertaining to Spring, or to Youth. The springtime of life.

VERNER, LINDA.—Appeared in the original production of *Trial by Jury* as the Plaintiff.

Victor Emmanuel (Pat. 1).—Mentioned in the Colonel's Song. Victor Emmanuel II, King of Sardinia, 1849–1861, and King of Italy, 1861–1878. He was universally popular.

VINCENT, RUTH.—Created the part of Gretchen in *The Grand Duke*. After playing lead in some of the revivals, she became one of the foremost opera and concert vocalists of the day.

Violoncello (*Jane is discovered leaning on a violoncello.* Stage Direction. Pat. 2).—This is usually replaced by a double bass, partly because a 'cello is not big enough for Lady Jane to lean on when standing up, partly because the authors were burlesquing the customary double bass accompaniments in Grand Opera recitatives.

Virelay ("In a whispered virelay." U. 2).—An ancient French song form in two rhymes.

Virtue of Necessity ("Then make a virtue of necessity." P.I. 2).—This expression is Shakespearean, taken from *Two Gentlemen of Verona*, Act IV, Scene 1. It is also to be found in the works of Chaucer, Rabelais, and Dryden.

Vittoria (G.).—One of the Contadine.

Viviparians ("You South Pacific Island viviparians." U. 1).—A living creature which produces its young alive instead of in the form of a pre-natal egg. As this applies to the human race, it has no special application to the Utopians, and is merely a convenient rhyme to "barbarians."

W

WALTON, LISA.—Appeared in the original production of *The Sorcerer* as Constance.

Wards.—Gilbert is fond of putting his young ladies under legal guardianship. All Major-General Stanley's daughters are wards in chancery (Pir.); Phyllis is also so (I.); while Yum-Yum, Pitti-Sing, and Peep-Bo are the wards of Ko-Ko (M.).

WARE, IRENE.—Appeared in the original production of *The Sorcerer* as Aline.

Warren the Preacher Poet (Y. 1).—One of Colonel Fairfax's fellow prisoners. See "Byfleet, Sir Martin."

WARWICK, GIULIA.—Created the part of Constance in *The Sorcerer*. Also appeared in the same original production as Aline. She became a professor of singing at the Guildhall School of Music.

Water from far Cologne (T. by J.).—Eau de Cologne. The original inventor was Johann Maria Farina, who founded his perfumery in Cologne. It is now made in France by his descendants, while similar scents are manufactured in England.

Waterford ("A smack of Lord Waterford, reckless and rollicky." Pat. 1).—From the Colonel's Song. The Beresfords, the family name of the Marquisate of Waterford, have a reputation for bravery, daring, and sportsmanship.

Waterloo House ("A Waterloo House young man." Pat. 2).—This building, in Cockspur Street near

Waterloo Place, was the business place of Messrs. Halling, Pearce, and Stone, mercers and drapers.

Watteau ("An existence *à la* Watteau." T. by J.).— The famous French artist (1684–1721), who was known chiefly for his paintings of the Fêtes Galantes type.

Weapons.—The following weapons are mentioned in the operas: arquebus (Y. 2); axe (P.I. 3); bludgeon (U. 1); bomb (G.D. 1); chassepôt rifle (Pir. 1); chopper (M. 1; R. 1); dagger (I. 2; M. 1; R. 2; Y. 1); dynamite (U. 1); falchion (G.D. 1); gun (G. 1); halbert (Y. 1); life preserver (Pir. 2); Mauser rifle (instead of chassepôt) (Pir. 1); Maxim gun (U. 1); Nordenfelt gun (U. 1); pistol (Pin. 1; Pir. 2; U. 1; G.D. 1); poniard (R. 2); rapier (U. 1); rifle (P.I. 3); sabre (M. 2); snickersee (M. 2); spear (I. 2); sword (Pir. 2; P.I. 3; R. 2; U. 1; G.D. 1).

Weazels ("Weazels at their slumbers they trepan." P.I. 2).—The saying, "You can never catch a weazel asleep," is from Neal's *Brother Jonathan*, 1825. See "Trepan."

Wednesday Nights ("The cherished rights you enjoy on Wednesday nights." I. 1).—Wednesday is the night of the week for moving resolutions by private members in the House of Commons, a privilege much appreciated by the "Back Benchers," whose voices are otherwise seldom heard. The night for introducing private members' Bills is Friday, but both nights are often commandeered by the Government when there is pressure of official business.

Wellington ("When Wellington thrashed Bonaparte."
  I. 2).—From Mountararat's Song. At Waterloo in
  1815. The members of the Cabinet were nearly
  all commoners at this time, and thus the House of
  Commons was practically supreme. The spelling of
  Bonaparte is quite correct, for Napoleon changed
  it thus from Buonaparte when First Consul.

WELLS, JOHN WELLINGTON (S.).—Family Sorcerer,
  whose aid is invoked by Alexis to administer a love
  potion to the entire inhabitants of the village of
  Ploverleigh.

Westminster Hall ("In Westminster Hall I danced a
  dance." T. by J.).—Previous to the opening of the
  new Royal Courts of Justice in the Strand, most
  High Court cases were heard in Westminster Hall.
  See "Chancery Lane."

"When at the worst, affairs will mend" (I. 2).—The
  original of this paraphrase of the well-known
  saying, "The darkest hour is before the dawn," is
  the old English proverb, "When bale (evil) is hext
  (highest), boot (good fortune) is next."

"Where a will is, there's a way" (I. 2).—The proverb,
  "Where there's a will, there's a way," is derived
  from George Herbert's "To him that wills, ways are
  not found wanting."

White Tower (Y. 1).—(*Fairfax and two others entering the
  White Tower*, Stage Direction.)—This is incorrect.
  They enter the Coldharbour Tower, where Fairfax
  is believed to be. There is no access from the White
  Tower to his cell.

WILBRAHAM, CHARLES.—Created the parts of Sir Gilbert, the 18th Baronet, in *Ruddigore*; of the First Yeoman in *The Yeomen of the Guard*; and of Annibale in *The Gondoliers*. Also appeared in the original production of *The Yeomen of the Guard* as Fairfax and Leonard Meryll.

WILKINSON, JOHN.—Succeeded George Grossmith as Jack Point in the original production of *The Yeomen of the Guard*.

Wilkinson, Mr. (U. 1).—The "celebrated English tenor," actually Utopian, who nightly burlesques the King in comic opera.

Willahalah Willaloo (I. 2).—Meaningless expressions of grief uttered by the Fairies on learning that Iolanthe is for the second time condemned to death.

WILLIS, PRIVATE (I.).—Of the Grenadier Guards. He is on sentry duty in the Palace Yard, and the Queen of the Fairies falls a victim to his martial bearing. In actual practice, there is no military guard attached to the Houses of Parliament.

WILSON, ETHEL.—Created the part of Elsa in *The Grand Duke*.

Windsor (Y. 1).—Where the Court is in residence, and from whence Leonard Meryll comes with a despatch for the Lieutenant of the Tower.

"Wink is oft as good as nod" (Pin. 2).—This is a reversal of the real proverb, which is, "A nod is good as a wink to a blind horse."

Wishing Cap (S. 1).—Various things were used in witchcraft for wishing, such as caps, bones, gates, hats, purses, rods, stones, etc. Dekker wrote in 1600, "I shall want no wishing cap."

WORKMAN, C. H.—Created the part of Ben Hashbaz in *The Grand Duke*. He subsequently became the leading comedian, following in turn Grossmith and Passmore, and played in all the later revivals. At the end of Mrs. D'Oyly Carte's tenancy of the Savoy Theatre in 1909, he became lessee for a time, producing Gilbert and German's *Fallen Fairies* and Reginald Somerville's *The Mountaineers*, the conductor of the last-named being the well-known Scottish composer, Hamish MacCunn, who died shortly afterwards. Workman then went to Australia with the D'Oyly Carte Colonial Company, and subsequently died on board ship.

"Worn-out garments show new patches" (Pin. 2).—This "proverb" is a paraphrase of the Biblical saying, "No man putteth a piece of new cloth into an old garment" (Mark iii. 21). It has so long been in common use that any sense of irreverence is needless.

WYATT, AGNES.—Appeared in the original production of *The Yeomen of the Guard* as Kate; and of *The Gondoliers* as Giulia, Fiametta, and Vittoria.

WYATT, FRANK.—Created the part of the Duke of Plaza-Toro in *The Gondoliers*. He appeared in no other Gilbert and Sullivan work, but made a great hit in George Dance and Edward Solomon's

The Nautch Girl at the Savoy, and in Gilbert and
Alfred Cellier's *The Mountebanks* at the old Lyric
Theatre. He and his wife, Violet Melnotte, built
and owned the Duke of York's Theatre (first called
the Trafalgar Square Theatre), and on his death,
his widow assumed sole proprietorship.

X

Xebeque (G. 1).—The boat in which the two Gondoliers sail to their island Kingdom of Barataria. It is a small, three-masted vessel, used in the Mediterranean for carrying merchandise.

Xeres ("Old Xeres we'll drink." G. 2).—The Spanish name for sherry, so-called from the town in Andalusia, where the wine is manufactured.

Y

YEOMAN, FIRST (Y.).—Also known as the Corporal.
He sings the solo in the opening chorus, and the
second verse of the couplets in praise of Fairfax
in the Finale to Act I. Curiously enough, it is the
Second Yeoman who is the tenor.

YEOMAN, FOURTH (Y.).—He and the Third
Yeoman, in the original production, sang a second
set of couplets in praise of Fairfax, but these have
since been omitted. These two characters do not
appear on the programme.

YEOMAN, SECOND (Y.).—He sings the first verse of
the couplets in praise of Fairfax in the Finale to
Act I.

YEOMAN, THIRD (Y.).—See "Yeoman, Fourth."

Yeomen of the Guard (Y.).—A personal bodyguard to
His Majesty. In Henry VIII's reign they were at
the Tower, as that was still for a time a Royal
residence. They are styled the King's Bodyguard of
the Yeomen of the Guard, and are stationed at St.
James's Palace. The Tower Warders are now a
separate corps, under the command of the Constable
of the Tower, and are known as Yeomen Warders.
Both corps are similarly uniformed in Tudor garb,
and, at the period of the story of the opera, were
practically identical, and resided within the precincts of the Tower of London.

YEOMEN OF THE GUARD, THE, or *THE
MERRYMAN AND HIS MAID*.—Tenth opera.

Produced at the Savoy Theatre, October 3, 1888, and ran till November 30, 1889, with a total of 423 performances. It was revived in 1897 and 1906, the aggregate number of performances being 699.

NOTES ON "THE YEOMEN OF THE GUARD"

The new-comers to the company at the original production were Geraldine Ulmar, Courtice Pounds, Wallace Brownlow, W. R. Shirley, and W. H. Denny. All of these, except the last-named, had already appeared previously at the Savoy, but this was the first time they created parts. Mr. Denny was engaged, as Rutland Barrington had left temporarily to embark on his own management.

The Overture was written by Sullivan in the auditorium during a final rehearsal, the half-dried parts being thrown to the instrumentalists as they were completed.

On Saturday, August 17, 1889, Grossmith bade farewell to Savoy Opera, and started his long and final career as a Society Entertainer who filled the whole programme. He had played without intermission since the production of *The Sorcerer*, and had been absent, through short holidays, illness, and bereavement, only sixty times out of a possible attendance of 4,616 performances.

The Introduction to Dame Carruthers' Song is a genuine example of the Wagnerian type of *leit motiv*, and reappears in the Finale to Act I both in the major and minor keys.

The blindfold marriage and the prisoner's escape resemble the situations in Wallace's *Maritana*.

The opera was intended originally to have a modern setting, but the sight of a warder on an advertisement suggested to the author the Tower of London in Tudor times.

Colonel Fairfax is the only male character who has three complete changes of costume, while Sir Richard Cholmondeley is the only real person in the operas.

There was originally a song for Sergeant Meryll in Act I, commencing "A laughing boy of yester- day."

The melody of "I have a song to sing O" is founded on an old sea shanty.

Courtice Pounds wore a moustache as the pseudo-warder. The Sergeant says merely that Fairfax "shall shave off his beard." The modern custom of making the Colonel, as a Yeoman, clean-shaved tends to render him too young- looking to be received into the Corps.

Youngest character.—Ignoring Frederic (Pir.), who, by birthdays, is only "five and a little bit over," the youngest characters whose ages are definitely stated are Constance (S.) and Elsie Maynard (Y.), each seventeen. Patience (Pat.) is eighteen, and Phyllis (I.) is nineteen. The youngest of the men are Frederic (Pir.) (reckoning by years) and Hilarion (P.I.), both twenty-one.

YUM-YUM (M.).—Ward of Ko-Ko, to whom she is betrothed.

Z

ZARA, PRINCESS (U.).—Eldest daughter of King Paramount, in love with Captain Fitzbattleaxe.

Zoffany ("I can tell undoubted Raphaels from . . . Zoffanies." Pir. 1).—Johann Zoffany, a German painter, who came to England in 1758, became an R.A. in 1769, and died at Kew in 1810. His speciality was portraits of actors in character. There is, therefore, some veiled humour in the Major-General's boast, for no two artists could differ more in style than Raphael and Zoffany.

ZORAH (R.).—One of the professional bridesmaids. Richard Dauntless, thrown over by Rose Maybud, consoles himself with her affections.

Zorah˘ (S.).—The Christian name of Mrs. Partlet.